Strategies for Implementing

INTEGRATED MARKETING COMMUNICATIONS

Strategies for Implementing

INTEGRATED

MARKETING

COMMUNICATIONS

Larry Percy

Printed on recyclable paper

American Marketing Association
Chicago, Illinois

 NTC Business Books
a division of *NTC Publishing Group* • Lincolnwood, Illinois USA

Library of Congress Cataloging-in-Publication Data

Percy, Larry.
    Strategies for implementing integrated marketing communications /
Larry Percy.
       p.   cm.
    Includes index.
    ISBN 0–8442–3583–0 (alk. paper)
    1. Communication in marketing.   I. Title.
HF5415.123.P476 1997
658.8′02—dc20   96-32075
                                                CIP

Credits for illustrations: See page 233, which is an extension of the copyright page.

Published in conjunction with the American Marketing Association, 250 South Wacker Drive, Chicago, Illinois 60606.

Published by NTC Business Books, a division of NTC Publishing Group
4255 West Touhy Avenue
Lincolnwood (Chicago), Illinois 60606-1975, U.S.A.
Manufactured in the United States of America.

6 7 8 9 0 BC 9 8 7 6 5 4 3 2 1

For Mary Walton

CONTENTS

This strategic planning process may seem simple enough, and you may even be thinking, "We do this already, or near enough." We agree that the logic is rather straightforward, but the implementation requires a great deal of attention and understanding. The next six chapters discuss in detail the many considerations necessary to ensure implementing a truly successful and effective integrated marketing communications program.

Planning Tools

To help organize your thinking as you work your way through this strategic planning process, we present a number of worksheets and grids. There are specific worksheets that incorporate questions that will help you link the target audience to both the marketing and communication strategies. The Behavioral Sequence Model[20] introduced in depth in Chapter 3 helps in understanding what is involved in the decision to purchase or use a brand or service. Drawing upon this model of the decision process, a grid we call the IMC Task Grid helps establish specific communication tasks for each important stage of the decision process. Finally, an IMC Media Budget Allocation Grid helps you organize how selected media are being used to correctly meet the communication objectives associated with the various communication tasks that make up the IMC campaign.

A Sustainable Competitive Advantage

It is critical for marketers to maintain as much control as they can over the communications that they initiate or influence. As Schultz and his colleagues put it in their book, the basic reason for integrated marketing communications is that marketing communications will be the only sustainable competitive advantage of marketing organizations in the 1990s and into the 21st century.[21] This is perhaps a rather extreme claim, but it is certain that marketers can control only a limited amount of the total information their target audiences gather and process about their brands. This in a nutshell is why IMC is so critical for all marketers in the 1990s and beyond. One's entire marketing communications program must be integrated, that is, *strategically planned*, to ensure maximum impact.

Chapter Notes

[1] D. E. Schultz, S. I. Tannenbaum, and R. F. Lauterborn, *Integrated Marketing Communications* (Lincolnwood, IL: NTC Business Books, 1993).

[2] D. E. Schultz, "Integrated Marketing Communications: Maybe Definition Is in the Point of View," *Marketing News*, January 18, 1993: 17.

[3] D. E. Schultz and P. Wang, "Real World Results," *Marketing Tools*, April/May 1994: 40–47.

[4] Definition offered by the American Association of Advertising Agencies Committee on Integrated Marketing Communications.

[5] C. Caywood, D. E. Schultz, and P. Wang, *Integrated Marketing Communications: A Survey of National Consumer Goods* (Evanston, IL: Department of Integrated Advertising/Marketing Communications, Northwestern University, 1991).

[6] T. R. Duncan and S. E. Everett, "Client Perceptions of Integrated Marketing Communications," *Journal of Advertising Research*, May/June 1993: 30–39.

[7] T. R. Duncan and C. Caywood, "The Concept, Process, and Evolution of Integrated Marketing Communication," in E. Thorson and J. Moore (Eds.), *Integrated Communication* (Mahwah, NJ: Lawrence Erlbaum Associates, 1996), 13–34.

[8] Report from Shearson-Lehman Hutton, *Diversification Begets Integration*, 1989.

[9] Reported in *Advertising Age*, January 25, 1993, 44.

[10] D. E. Schultz, "Traditional Advertising Has Role to Play in IMC," *Marketing News*, August 28, 1995: 18.

[11] D. E. Schultz, "What Is Direct Marketing," *Journal of Direct Marketing* 9(2) (1995), 5–9.

[12] J. R. Rossiter and L. Percy, *Advertising Communications and Promotion Management* (New York: McGraw-Hill, 1997).

[13] Data are compiled from information in "Marketer's Guide to Media," *ADWEEK* 17(1) (1994), 9–12 and "Steady Growth Seen in Ad Spending over Five Years," *Marketing News*, September 11, 1995: 3.

[14] "Marketer's Guide to Media," *ADWEEK* 17(1) (1994), 9–12.

[15] Reported in "Integrated Marketing? It's Synergy," *Advertising Age*, March 8, 1993: 22.

[16] E. Thorson and J. Moore, "Introduction," in E. Thorson and J. Moore (Eds.), *Integrated Communication* (Mahaw, NJ: Lawrence Erlbaum Associates, 1966), 1–10.

[17] J. Moore and E. Thorson, "Strategic Planning for Integrated Marketing Communications Programs: An Approach to Moving from Chaotic towards Systematic," in E. Thorson and J. Moore (Eds.), *Integrated Communication* (Mahaw, NJ: Lawrence Erlbaum Associates, 1966), 135–152.

[18] Rossiter and Percy, *Advertising Communications and Promotion Management*.

[19] Ibid.

[20] Ibid.

[21] Schultz, Tannenbaum, and Lauterborn, *Integrated Marketing Communications*.

Initial IMC Planning Considerations

Before we can even begin to think about the many options available for delivering a marketing communication message, we must have a plan. Whom do we wish to communicate with, and what effect do we wish our communications to have on them? These questions are at the heart of IMC planning (or any communication strategy, for that matter).

Target Audience Considerations

The first step in communication planning is to decide upon the target audience. As with most things, this is usually not as easy as it seems. From a *marketing* standpoint this is very important, but we assume this decision has been made as part of the marketing plan before we begin to work out a communication strategy. Target markets or target audiences are generally identified in terms of market segments. In IMC planning, therefore, we know which segments of our market we wish to address.

What we need to determine is what our market looks like in terms of potential buyer or user groups. Do we want to talk to people who are customers or possible new users? Again, these questions are usually answered at a general level by the marketing plan. But the answer to this question determines whether our basic communication strategy will be to drive trial or repeat purchase. As we shall see below, there are important tactical considerations associated with how we address these two groups.

Most marketers want to go beyond this basic division between customers and non-customers and further divide their target audience. For example, customers can be highly loyal to one brand, or simply use the same brand regularly because they haven't found one they like better. As you might imagine, it would be very important to understand which of these two attitudes toward your product or service your customers held.[1] Your customers could also use your brand more or less exclusively, or use it interchangeably among others.

We can look at non-customers in much the same way. Non-customers may simply not use any product or service in the category. Those who do may have tried but rejected your brand; others may simply not be aware of it. Non-customers may be highly loyal to one brand or company, or they may switch among alternatives, although they do not include your brand.

As we have said, nothing is ever as simple as it seems at first glance. For our discussions, we are going to look at customers and non-customers in terms of the five prospective buyer groups described by Rossiter and Percy.[2] They look at potential target audiences in terms of three non-customer groups: new category users, other-brand loyals, and other-brand switchers; and two customer groups: favorable brand switchers and brand loyals as shown in Figure 2.1. Non-customers include those who have never purchased or used *any* product or service on the category (new category users), those who are loyal to a competitor brand (other-brand loyals), and those who switch among brands, but do not include our brand in their set (other-brand switchers). Customers are either loyal to our brand (brand loyals) or buy or use our brand along with competitors (brand switchers).

Figure 2.1
Five Potential Target Audience Groups

Non-Customer Groups:	New Category Users
	Other-Brand Loyals
	Other-Brand Switchers
Customer Groups:	Favorable Brand Switchers
	Brand Loyals

Linking the Target Audience to Marketing Strategy

If our marketing objective is to increase trial, we will need to communicate with non-customers. If our marketing objective is to generate repeat business, we will need to communicate with customers. These distinctions will hold whether we are addressing a consumer, business, or trade audience. Regardless of the target audience, we generally want them to take some kind of "action," and this is almost always a variation of these two basic buyer behaviors: trial or repeat purchase, or use.

Consumer Target Objectives. Trial objectives for consumer target audiences center on stimulation of retail outlet visits or mail, phone, or personal sales inquiries in the case of a high price product or service, and direct trial of a product or service in the case of less involving fast turnover consumer products. Repeat purchase objectives for consumers include increasing the rate at which a brand is used and favorable recommendations to others, in addition to simply continuing to purchase.

Business Target Objectives. The trial action objectives for business target audiences can include generation of inquiries about a new product or service, requests for feasibility studies, product demonstrations, or initial quotations. The repeat purchase action objectives are aimed at current customers to encourage them to use us more often as a supplier, buy more of our product or service than at present, refer us to other prospective customers, or simply to remain loyal by continuing to buy our product or service as they are doing at present.

Trade Target Objectives. The trial action objectives for trade target audiences (wholesalers or retailers) focus on persuading them to carry and stock our product or offer our service. The repeat action objectives refer to the trade's in-outlet promotion of our product by allocating it good shelf space, placing special displays, and having sales personnel recommend our product or service to customers.

The trade, in turn, have buyers as their target. Sometimes these buyers are the same ultimate target market that the marketer is seeking (as in manufacturer's brands sold through grocery and drug stores that carry their own "private label" brands—a growing trend). While trade's and manufacturers' action objectives are the same at the brand level, the trade is more broadly interested in store or outlet trial, and store or outlet repeat patronage.

Linking the Target Audience to Communication Strategy

Now that we have looked at what we expect our target audience to do, it is time to see how advertising and promotion help meet these trial and repeat purchase or usage "action" objectives. This will be our first look at how important it is to understand the relevant behavior of the members of our target audience. In the next chapter we will be introducing the Behavioral Sequence Model, a planning tool that helps you look at this question in a great deal of detail. At this point however, we need to briefly introduce you to one aspect of the Behavioral Sequence Model—the *roles* people play in the decision to buy or use a product or service.

The roles people play in making a decision are very important to understand because marketing communication should be designed to influence individuals in particular decision roles. We can imagine at least five roles that people could play that will have a direct effect upon their response to our communication:

1. *Initiator*: the person who gets the overall purchase decision started. The aim of marketing communication here is to have this person *propose* our brand or service.

2. *Influencer*: someone who uses information about what we are offering to either advance or hinder the decision to purchase or use our brand. We want this person to *recommend* our brand or service.

3. *Decider*: the person who makes the actual "go/no go" decision. We want this person to *choose* our brand or service.

4. *Purchaser*: this person actually executes the decision. We, of course, want this person to *buy* our brand or service.

5. *User*: often overlooked, the person who actually uses the product or service is part of the decision process. We want this person to *use* our brand or service and our communications to the user should help form and solidify positive attitudes toward it.

An important point to understand here is that our specific marketing communication objectives will differ depending upon which decision role we are addressing. Also, we need to know who and how many people are involved in each role. It is quite possible that a single person will fill all five roles; or a number of people may be involved with each role, as is especially likely with business or trade target audiences. We will have more to say about this in the next chapter.

What we want to do now is consider how marketing communications can be used tactically to address trial and repeat purchase or usage objectives for the different roles various members of our target audience could play in a purchase or usage decision. At this point too we will be making a distinction between traditional advertising and promotion, the two primary components of marketing communications. This will be our first look at how either advertising or promotion might be a better choice in a particular situation to satisfy a particular objective.

Trial Objective for Advertising and Promotion. Advertising or promotion to generate trial is usually aimed at one or more of the first three decision roles—initiator, influencer, or decider—depending upon with whom the critical decisions affecting trial of our product or service reside. In the next section we will be looking at specific communication effects for advertising and promotion. Here we are taking a more general look by way of introduction.

For any target audience, we must consider which role is being targeted, and what decision needs to be influenced by the communication. Is the consumer aware of us? Perhaps we are not yet on the initial vendor or product consideration list for a business target audience; or perhaps we are not yet thought of favorably enough by the trade to be widely distributed. As we shall see, advertising could help deal with these problems by raising awareness or creating a favorable attitude.

Promotions are widely used to stimulate trial. In fact, most new products are launched with at least as much expenditure on promotion as on advertising, and usually more when expenditure on distributor or retailer promotion is considered. For business target audiences, trial promotions are most frequently some type of product demonstration or service sampling in some form, for example at trade shows, in-house demonstrations, or free or low-cost trial periods under warranty. For distributor target audiences, trial promotions nearly always are financial, for example trade allowances, co-op advertising contributions, sales staff contests, and the like. For consumer target audiences, trial promotions are quite specialized and will be dealt with in some detail in Chapter 5.

Repeat Purchase Objective for Advertising and Promotion. Advertising or promotion used to increase repeat purchase is usually aimed at the purchaser role (for example to buy a larger size or place a bigger order) or the user role (to use our product or service more often or in larger amounts during usage or consumption occasions). Advertising to increase usage must often concentrate on "re-awareness," for example in an office or home usage situation where the users must be reminded to use what they already have on hand. Additionally, of course, the advertising message usually must provide reasons for increased usage. Campaigns demonstrating long-run usage opportunities are good examples of usage advertising. A good example is an extended usage campaign for baking soda where consumers are encouraged to keep an open box in the refrigerator and to occasionally empty one down the drain.

Repeat purchase promotions are usually employed to increase the buyers' usage of the brand by either getting them to buy more often over the long term or purchase more in the short term. Generally, the primary purpose of repeat purchase promotions should be to increase the *rate* at which a product or service is purchased or used. For business target audiences, continuity programs or loyalty incentives help to protect current customers from competitors' offerings. Repeat purchase promotions for consumer target audiences are often specifically designed to increase usage rather than to attract new trial as such. Good examples would include "bounce-back" coupons good for future purchase instead of trial coupons, or multiple-purchase rebates instead of a single-purchase rebate. The main strength of promotion is to get favorable brand switchers (customers) to select us more often from among the set of alternative products or services they use. With trade target audiences, volume purchase discounts, co-op advertising contributions, and sales contests or bonus incentives can be employed.

Repeat purchase promotions work primarily on brand purchase intention, a communication effect which we shall see in the next section is a particular strength of promotion over advertising. They are usually aimed at switchers in order to lure them from alternatives by offering the best deal on a particular purchase occasion. Despite the focus on brand purchase intention, some repeat purchase promotions have the potential to increase favorable attitudes toward a product or service, so that in some circumstances, this could lead to a stronger position for the brand among switchers in the target audience's acceptable set and perhaps increase the chances of their becoming a brand loyal. However, the reality of most repeat purchase promotions is that they mainly alter the timing of purchases through manipulating brand purchase intentions. Repeat purchase promotions "buy" customers when the promotion is on, then lose them when it's off. Repeat purchase promotions are therefore effective in meeting short-term competitive threats. Long-term success depends much more on good advertising and wide penetration (trial) promotions than on repeat purchase promotions.

In this section we have introduced the first step in IMC planning, looking at the target audience in terms of marketing and communication strategy. What we have seen is that there is more to customers and non-customers than this simple dichotomy, and that these differences have important implications for marketing communications. We have also seen that the two primary components of marketing communications, traditional advertising and promotion, address these differences with unique strengths. It is these unique strengths that demand an integrated approach to communications planning, and lead to IMC.

Next, we shall examine in much more detail some of the unique strengths of advertising and promotion in terms of communication effects.

Relative Communication Strengths of Advertising and Promotion

All aspects of integrated marketing communication work on the same basic communications effects[3]: category need, brand awareness, brand attitude, and brand purchase intention. It should be noted that while we use the term "brand" to describe these effects, we are using the word in its broadest possible sense to include products, services, corporate identity—in short, whatever might be the beneficiary of our marketing communication.

Often in marketing we find that there are particular problems that we must address that lie outside the main thrust of our marketing communication. For example, we may have introduced a new product and found it so successful that sales outstripped production. This is a "problem" we might all like to have, but if one is not careful it could really become a problem. Potential customers, disappointed at not being able to find the product, might form negative attitudes, or almost certainly look for an alternative. With a seldom-purchased product this could take a lot of people out of the market. Because situations like this do occur occasionally, a fifth "catch-all" communication effect is included to deal with them: purchase facilitation. In our example we might want to alert the market that because the product is so good we are having a hard time meeting demand, but that the problem is solved and more product will be available within a few weeks.

Before we examine the relative strength of traditional advertising and promotion in generating these five communication effects, we shall briefly review each of them (see Figure 2.2).

Figure 2.2
Five Basic Communication Effects

Basic Communication Effect	Description
Category Need	Target audience perception they require a product or service to satisfy a need
Brand Awareness	Target audience ability to recognize or recall the product or service
Brand Attitude	Target audience overall evaluation of product or service in relation to its ability to satisfy the reason they want it
Brand Purchase Intention	Target audience instruction to themselves to respond to the product or service offered
Purchase Facilitation	Target audience perception that some marketing factor could affect their purchase or use of the product or service

Category need: This is the target audience's perception that they require a product or service to satisfy a need. In other words, they must "be in the market" for whatever we are offering.

Brand awareness: While this is obviously the target audience's ability to recognize what we are offering, there is an important distinction between *recognition* awareness and *recall* awareness. In the case of recognition, the potential customer need only recognize the brand at the point of purchase; with recall, they must recall or remember the brand name when the need for the product or service occurs.

Brand attitude: This refers to the target audience's overall evaluation of the product or service we are offering in relation to its perceived ability to satisfy the reason they want it (the relevant motivation, as we shall see). It is important to remember that reasons for purchase or usage can differ at various times, even for the same individual. That is why we must always think about brand attitude in terms of motivations that are likely to be driving behavior when our target audience is "in the market."

Brand purchase intention: This is the target audience's instruction to themselves to purchase or use what we are offering. In other words, it is a commitment to take action, but it does *not* ensure actually purchasing or using our brand.

Purchase facilitation: As described above, this is the target audience's perception that some marketing factor could affect their purchase or use of our brand. These factors could include product-related issues, price, or distribution.

As you might gather, even from these brief descriptions, there is a lot involved with these communication effects that we must consider in IMC planning. It is not enough to simply say we want people to like our brand; or that we want people to use it more often. We need to look carefully at what it will take to accomplish those ends, and what type of advertising and/or promotion will best do the job.

In general, the relative communication strengths of the promotion and advertising components of marketing communications are depicted in Figure 2.3. The promotion aspects of marketing communications generally make their strongest contributions to brand awareness and brand purchase intention. The advertising components generally make their strongest contribution to brand awareness and brand attitude. However, while brand attitude is not one of the strengths of promotion, the best promotion offers will still be those that also work on brand attitude. These promotions are what Prentice has called *consumer franchise building*[4] promotion offers, and which we think of in terms of brand equity. This is something we will examine in more detail later in Chapter 5 when we look specifically at promotions and how to use them to reinforce brand equity.

We must also bear in mind that promotion alone, as well as advertising alone, can actually create all five communication effects. Store brands and so-called "price brands" are marketed successfully without advertising by using point-of-purchase promotions, although there is now a trend toward advertising even private label and store brands. Promotion, like advertising, works through communication, and either one can perform all the communications tasks. But as we are seeing, the whole idea of integrated marketing communications is to approach one's communications tasks with an open mind, and to explore all marketing communications

Figure 2.3
Relative Communication Strengths of Advertising and Promotion

Communication Objective	Weak / Strong bars	Communication Strengths
Category Need		*Promotion:* helps accelerate need *Advertising:* suggests category
Brand Awareness		*Promotion:* strong recognition *Advertising:* strong recognition and recall
Brand Attitude		*Promotion:* potentially good if re-inforces brand equity *Advertising:* traditional strength
Brand Purchase Intention		*Promotion:* traditional strength *Advertising:* some, especially retail
Purchase Facilitation		*Promotion:* some, but costly *Advertising:* limited unless inno-vative

options in order to maximize the brand message to the target audience. The relative strengths of advertising and promotion are discussed next for each of the five communication effects.

Category Need

Category need, for most product categories, originates mainly from cultural changes (for new categories) and arises from a person's overall or temporary circumstances (for new and existing categories). Traditional advertising can have some effect on category need by selling a category. However, selling the category is more a matter of suggesting the category. If there is not an underlying motive to be tapped, "selling" will be all but impossible. For example, the successful introduction of passenger "mini-vans" by Chrysler would not have been possible if there was not an already reasonably strong motivation to purchase such a practical vehicle. Only rarely can advertising create a motivation as such. Rather, it positions the category as a better way of meeting an existing motivation. In the case of mini-vans, it was the motivation of "incomplete satisfaction" with alternatives for family transportation. We will have more to say about motivation and its importance later.

Various forms of promotion can help accelerate category need, make it occur earlier, although usually only to a fairly minor degree. This is one of the reasons couponing and price promotions are almost always a part of new consumer product introductions, and why direct marketing as a means of delivering a very targeted promotion can play such an important role in the introduction of an innovative service or product for business. Accelerate is the key term here. None of this really sells the category need so much as it attempts to speed it up.

Overall, both the advertising and promotion components of marketing communications have, in general, only a relatively minor influence on category need (as we see in Figure 2.3). Again, this is only a general effect, for one may certainly find that specific instances of successfully selling or accelerating category need with either advertising or promotional techniques do occur.

Brand Awareness

Brand awareness is one of the strengths of traditional advertising. However, almost any form of marketing communications can be a contributor to brand awareness to at least some extent. New product introductions, when brand awareness is a major objective, typically utilize several marketing communications tools.

Promotion offers help prospective buyers to consider new brands and to reconsider existing brands. Promotion offers achieve this by drawing reflexive attention to the brand (for example, a point-of-purchase display or a sample pack) and also by producing selective attention (for example, price-off or coupons promising extra value).

Various promotions and most messages (whether promotion or advertising) delivered through direct marketing are primarily useful for increasing brand recognition at the point of purchase or at the point of decision rather than stimulating brand recall prior to purchase (although this is possible). As a result, promotions and direct marketing are less often an option when brand recall is involved.

Brand Attitude

Brand attitude communication historically is the province of advertising. However, as we have already pointed out, all marketing communications should work on brand attitude. Unfortunately, most promotions are aimed primarily at causing a short-term increase in sales, for competitive or inventory moving reasons, without regard to brand attitude. But the ideal communication should always help create longer term communications effects. This is especially true for promotions, where this long-term effect is important in order to maximize full-value purchases when the promotion is withdrawn.

Consumer franchise building promotions as described by Prentice, or as we shall consider them, any promotions that pay attention to consistently reinforcing a brand's equity, contribute to inducing full-price purchases by working, like advertising, on brand attitude (for example, free samples). Short-term promotions too often do not affect brand attitude, but operate instead on temporary brand purchase intention (for example, price-off offers). But even here it is not impossible to interject some reinforcement of brand attitude. Let's look at the Ginkai FSI in Figure 2.4. The headline of the insertion reads "Introducing Ginkai™ Ginkgo . . . Proven to Improve Memory and Concentration." The copy then goes on to provide support for the claims. Figure 2.5 details the coupons from this insertion. Notice that on this coupon, in addition to the picture of the package to reinforce brand recognition at the point of purchase, we find the headline repeated, as well as the tag line, "When it comes to Gingko...Think Ginkai™," all of which reinforces the brand attitude communication effect from the message. Additionally, all of this copy echoes the print and broadcast advertising for the brand, adding even more equity reinforcement (see Figure 2.6).

Chuck Mittelstadt, a long-time consultant to the Interpublic Group of Companies (the group that owns the three large agencies McCann-Erickson, Ammirati Puris Lintas, and Lowe), has offered an interesting observation on this subject. He points out that years ago image-building promotions were the norm. Among others, there were such classic promotions as the Pillsbury bake-off and the launch of White Rain hair-care products. The Pillsbury bake-off he sees as a classic example of IMC. The bake-off stands for well-crafted quality products and constant innovation. As a result, this promotion was a major contributor to the Pillsbury brand image.

For the introduction of White Rain, a young woman (consistent with the demographics of the target audience) dressed in a white raincoat and white boots and holding a white umbrella was used as the most prominent element on the package. Models dressed in the same fashion were used to

Figure 2.4
A Promotion Offer Designed to Increase Brand Recognition

dispense free samples. They used white raincoats and umbrellas as premiums and as point-of-purchase displays. The advertising spokeswoman was dressed the same, and the copy stressed the widely accepted folklore on the softness of rainwater. The brand lives today on that integrated imagery.

Unfortunately, too often today many package goods brand managers lean too heavily upon short-term price promotions to help reach sales objectives, and are injuring brand equity. The proof of this may be seen in the overwhelming allotment of promotion dollars given to the trade, where half the money is kept by the trade and the rest usually passed along to

Figure 2.5
A Coupon That Reinforces Brand Recognition and Brand Attitude

consumers by way of price-off "specials." As Mittelstadt puts it, somewhere along the line marketers took a shortcut into price promotions as a way of life, and a lot of brands are now paying dearly for it.

Brand Purchase Intention

Brand purchase intention has historically been the communication strength of the promotion component of marketing communication. With the exception of retail advertising and other direct response advertising, most

Figure 2.6
Print Ad That Works with Other Promotions to Reinforce Brand Equity

traditional advertising does not deal directly with brand purchase intention. However, all promotion, and most messages delivered through direct marketing and channels marketing, are aimed at "moving sales forward" immediately (too often, as noted above, regardless of their longer-term consequences), and they achieve this by stimulating immediate brand purchase intention. More particularly, promotions stimulate intention to buy

Figure 2.7
Incidence of Point-of-Purchase Brand Choices for Supermarket Products

Type of Choice	Percentage of Purchases
Overall Results	
Specifically planned brand choice	34
Point-of-purchase brand choice	<u>66</u>
	100
Types of Point-of-Purchase Brand Choices	
Generally planned (category but not brand)	10
Substitute (switched from intended brand)	3
Impulse (neither category or brand intended)	<u>53</u>
	66
Point-of-Purchase Brand Choice for Specific Products	
Candy and gum	85
Snack foods	83
Cereal	68
Laundry aids/supplies	61
Soft drinks	59
Fresh meat, poultry, fish	51
Baby foods/baby needs	49
Magazines/newspapers	29

Source: 1994 POPAI study of consumer buying habits

now, or to buy more than usual, as well as the many purchase-related intentions for consumer durables and industrial products such as intention to visit showrooms, call for a sales demonstration, and so forth.

Dramatic evidence of the opportunity for promotions to influence brand purchase intention for consumer products comes from the ongoing Point-of-Purchase Advertising Institute (POPAI) studies of consumer buying habits.[5] On average, 66 percent of the final brand choices for supermarket items are made at the point of purchase (Figure 2.7). Although the incidence varies by product category from a low of about 50 percent for such things as fresh meat, poultry and fish, or baby food, to a high in the mid 80 percent range for snacks and magazines or newspapers, it is clear that for almost every category in the supermarket there is an opportunity for brand purchase intention to be influenced by promotion at the point of purchase.

Of further interest is that 53 percent of choices, overall, are so-called impulse purchases, where the category itself was not planned before entering the store. Most of these choices, we believe, are not purely impulse but rather reflect brand recognition reminding shoppers of a category need. Nevertheless, for the probable 10 percent or so of pure impulse choices, point-of-purchase presentation can be credited with generating all prior communication effects up to and including brand purchase intention.

Purchase Facilitation

Traditional advertising, unless it is particularly innovative, generally has a limited influence on purchase facilitation, especially if there is a severe problem with the rest of the marketing mix that, because of poor planning, has been left for the advertising to try to solve. Purchase facilitation problems with the product, price, or distribution can more often be overcome with other forms of marketing communications, though at considerable cost.

Promotions, emphasizing a severe price reduction, can sometimes sell a poor product. Promotions along price lines can also, at least temporarily, solve an overpricing problem. Direct marketing can help overcome poor distribution. All these are costly corrections, however, to marketing mix problems that should not have been left to promotion. In some cases, as we shall see later when we discuss it in more detail, channels marketing can help facilitate purchase because it is customized to more manageable marketing areas.

The Importance of Brand Awareness and Brand Attitude

Depending upon our specific objectives, we may wish to accomplish any of the five communication effects. However, regardless of our overall objectives, we will *always* want to stimulate awareness for our product or service, and to positively contribute to its equity, with every piece of our marketing communication.[6] As a result, brand awareness and brand attitude will always be an important part of IMC planning. Although we have briefly introduced these effects, because of their critical nature, it will pay to explore each of them in more detail.

Brand Awareness as an Objective

Almost any marketer if asked if awareness is important, is certain to say "yes." But how often have you seen an advertisement or promotion, and not noticed who the sponsor was? In fact, it is not unusual to talk about a funny or unique commercial in some detail, yet not be able to identify the advertiser! I am sure you are probably thinking of an example or two now. How could this happen?

One of the biggest dangers in creating marketing communications is the assumption that the target audience is going to "get" the message. It is an easy and understandable trap to fall into. When it is your brand and you have spent a great deal of time and energy on an advertising or promotion execution, *you* certainly know what the brand is, and what you are trying to communicate. Unfortunately, your target audience has not been involved in the creation of the ad or promotion; and they do not spend most of their waking hours thinking about the brand.

As a result, simply mentioning the brand name will not guarantee brand awareness. We must carefully think about where and how awareness of the brand will feature in the purchase or use of our product or service by the target audience. What we are after is to provide the target audience with sufficient detail to identify the brand within the category at the time the decision to purchase or use is made. It may even be that sufficient detail does not require the identification of the brand name as such. Often it is no more than a visual image of the package that a consumer uses to identify a brand.

Under other circumstances, it may not be necessary to recall a brand name. If the buyer does not "think aloud" about a specific brand, and simply waits until he or she sees and recognizes it at the point of purchase, then brand awareness does not require recall prior to purchase. Of course, there are many cases when the buyer does need to recall a brand prior to purchase. Understanding these differences in brand awareness are extremely important to IMC planning. Brand *recognition* and brand *recall* are two distinct types of brand awareness, and which one to use depends upon which communication effect occurs first in the mind of the target audience. Does a category need occur and the buyer look for a product or service to meet it, or does the buyer see the product and remember the need?

Recognition Awareness. In a number of purchase situations, it is really seeing the brand itself in the store and recognition of the brand that reminds the consumer of the category need: is this something I need or want? What goes on in the consumer's mind in terms of our communication effects is: *Brand awareness (in terms of recognition) reminds the consumer of category need.* This brand recognition can be either visual or verbal. In the store, merely seeing the package may key awareness of the brand. On the other hand, especially with telemarketing, *hearing* the brand name may key brand awareness. In either event, it is the recognition of the brand that constitutes the awareness, even though it may actually fail a recall test.

As an example of what we mean, think about how people shop in supermarkets. Market research consistently shows that very few shoppers actually use lists; and those who do will only have category reminders rather than brand names (e.g., bread, detergent, etc.). What happens is that as shoppers move up and down the aisles, when scanning the shelves they recognize brands (usually the package) and mentally decide if they need it or not.

What does this tell us about our marketing communications? When brand awareness is likely to be recognition, we need to be sure our communications include a strong representation of the brand as it will be confronted at the point of purchase. This means large visuals of the package for most packaged goods products (in the advertising, on coupons, etc.), and repetition of the brand name for products likely to be sold or solicited over the telephone.

Recall Awareness. In many purchase or usage decision-making situations, the brand is not available as a cue. The customer first experiences a need, and then thinks of potential solutions Here the product or service must already be stored in the mind of the target audience. But more than that, it must also be "linked" in the target audience's mind with the category need. Just knowing the brand is not enough. It must be made *salient* so that it is recalled from among the many brands people may be aware of when they are ready to make a decision.

As an example, if you were read a list of restaurants in your area, you would probably recognize most of them. However, when you decide to go out to eat, only two or three will come to mind, and you will make your selection from these. If you own an Italian restaurant, you want people to think of you when they think of eating out at an Italian restaurant. It doesn't help if your target audience is "aware" of you when cued (recognition awareness); they must *recall* you when the appropriate need occurs. What must happen in the consumer's mind in terms of our communication effects is: *Category need (what he or she wants) reminds the consumer of brand awareness.* To achieve this sequence of effects it is important that your advertising and promotion strongly associate the category need with your brand name. Ideally, this link will be repeated often in order to seat the relationship in the target audience's mind.

Brand Attitude

The issue of brand attitude is an involved one, and beyond the scope of this book. Nevertheless, a general understanding is essential for effective IMC planning. We will take as our model the Rossiter-Percy Grid,[7] which looks at marketing communication brand attitude strategy in terms of two critical dimensions: involvement and motivation.

Involvement. It is generally acknowledged today that the level of consumer involvement in choosing a product or service will affect the choice, and that this is probably a function of the complexity of the attitudes held toward a particular product or service. Without going into the research that underlies this, we will simply define involvement in terms of the psychological or financial risk perceived by the target audience in the purchase or use of our brand. In low involvement situations, trial experience will be sufficient because little or no risk is seen if the outcome is not positive. With high involvement choices, there will be definitely perceived risk in purchasing or using the product or service.

An important point to remember here is that perceived risk is in the eye of the consumer. It will always be important to "check the obvious," and be certain that there is or is not a perceived risk in the mind of your target audience. It is also good to remember that this perceived risk could vary by situation, even for the same person. For example, the choice of what wine to serve at a routine family meal may entail little risk, but the perceived risk could certainly increase when important guests are dining.

Motivation. Psychologists seem to agree that everything humans do is driven by a small set of motives. Of course, they don't all agree on exactly what constitutes that set of motives, but in general there is not a great deal of difference. Again to keep things simple, we will be looking only at a distinction between negative motives and positive motives. The interested reader is encouraged to read the Rossiter and Percy text. (See Figure 2.8 for a description of motivations considered by Rossiter and Percy).

The important point here to understand is that the reason why someone wants something, the motivation, causes attitudes to be formed in the first place. As a result, these motivations "energize" the purchase or usage decision. In one sense it is like a circle. The consumer is motivated to buy something and choose a particular brand because his or her attitude toward that brand suggests it is the best solution to satisfying that motivation. With purchase and usage, the attitude based upon the motive is strengthened with a good experience (or weakened with a bad experience).

To illustrate, if you have a bad headache, you will be motivated to do something about it (the negative motivation of problem-solution). You consider Advil the strongest and fastest-working brand of pain reliever (the attitude associated with the motive), and take some. The headache goes away, and the attitude-motive link is strengthened. But motives are specific to attitudes. Continuing our example, if you have a sinus headache,

---

Figure 2.8
Basic Motivations for Purchase Behavior

BASIC MOTIVE	DESCRIPTION
Negative Motives	
Problem Removal	Looking for product or service to *solve* a problem
Problem Avoidance	Looking for product or service to *avoid* a future problem
Incomplete Satisfaction	Looking for product or service that is *better* than what is currently used
Mixed Approach-Avoidance	Looking for product or service that *resolves* a combination of likes and dislikes in what is currently used
Normal Depletion	Looking to *maintain* inventory of product or ensure usage of service
Positive Motives	
Sensory Gratification	Looking to *enjoy* product or service
Intellectual Stimulation	Looking to *explore or master* a new product or service
Social Approval	Looking for *personal recognition* by using a product or service

---

Source: Rossiter and Percy, 1987

while the general motive remains the same (problem-solution), the attitudes associated with *sinus* headaches may lead to the choice of another brand such as Sinutab.

This example shows not only how attitudes are dependent upon motives, but how brand choices are linked to motives *via* attitudes. It also serves as a good example of how the brand awareness link must be carefully established. If your target audience makes a distinction between types of pain (i.e., their attitudes differ toward pain and hence toward brands), you must be sure the link between category need and brand awareness forged in your marketing communications reflects these attitudes.

The Rossiter-Percy Grid and Brand Attitude. Given these dimensions of involvement and motivation, a grid that reflects the interaction of the two easily follows. In effect, we are saying that if the fundamental criteria affecting product or service choice are the amount of perceived risk in the outcome of the decision and whether the need to be satisfied by the choice is negatively or positively motivated, then IMC planning must take into account the combination of involvement and motivation evidenced by the target audience.

These strategic quadrants are represented by the "grid" shown in Figure 2.9. Each of the four quadrants reflects a different strategic direction, either for low involvement/informational, low involvement/transformational, high involvement/informational, or high involvement/transformational decisions. The labels "informational" and "transformational" are used to describe strategies related to motivation in order to avoid confusion with the more psychologically correct terms of negative and positive. Generally, to satisfy a negative motive someone is seeking "information" about a brand in order to reduce or eliminate a problem, hence informational strategies. On the other hand, when positive motives are involved, someone is generally trying to "transform" themselves, so strategies dealing with positive motives are referred to as transformational.

Before going further, we need to caution the reader that the Rossiter-Percy Grid is *not* the same as the FCB advertising planning grid with which the reader may be familiar.[8] That grid too uses involvement (although defined differently), but also uses a second dimension called "think-feel." The two should not be confused. Actually, the full Rossiter-Percy Grid also includes an overlay of the brand recognition-brand recall distinction. But even when we look at the brand attitude component we have been discussing, there are significant strategic planning advantages.

What are the strategic implications for IMC planning suggested by the four quadrants of the brand attitude grid? Depending upon where your brand's purchase or usage decision lies within the grid, marketing commu-

Figure 2.9
Rossiter and Percy Brand Attitude Quadrants

		TYPE OF MOTIVATION	
		Informational (Negative motivations)	**Transformational** (Positive motivations)
	Low Involvement (Trial experience sufficient)		
TYPE OF DECISION	**High Involvement** (Search and conviction required prior to purchase)		

nication tactics will differ significantly. For example, when a decision implies no risk, you do not really need to convince the target audience. All you need do is titillate, or create what Maloney has called "curious disbelief."[9] This opens up your choice of media for delivering the message. On the other hand, with high involvement decisions you will need to convince. This means more permanent media (as opposed, say, to a 15-second commercial) should be considered.

We also know that when dealing with positive versus negative motives, an "emotional authenticity" is required in transformational executions. The target audience must sense that the feelings displayed are real and not contrived. This too will have significance for IMC planning. One of the reasons advertising is generally more effective than promotion for brand attitude is the broader availability of broadcast, especially television, to advertising. Of all the means of delivering marketing communications, television offers the greatest opportunity for eliciting emotional responses, as well as an advantage in portraying a sequence of emotions. All of this means television has built-in advantages for delivering transformational strategies that tap positive motives.

This does not mean that television, and hence advertising, is the only way to deal with transformational strategies. We have already mentioned that promotions can address brand attitude, and this means those associated with positive as well as negative motivations. In fact, when we look more specifically at various types of promotions in Chapter 5 we will see how they can be used to reinforce brand attitude. But having said this, when confronted with products or services that are associated with positive motives (motivations of sensory gratification, intellectual stimulation, and social approval), advertising should be used more often than not.

When dealing with negative motives and informational strategies, one has a lot more latitude. Here the basic task is to communicate information that supplies the "answer" to the need driven by one of the five negative motives. It is a lot easier to develop promotions that supply information than it is to create promotions that stimulate "emotional authenticity." While an emotional response is desired, even with informational strategies, to help energize the motivation, it is a lot less critical to the acceptance of the message.

This is a very important point that bears closer study if your brand falls into one of the two transformational quadrants.[10] For now, it is enough to remember that while promotions may be appropriate for some short-term tactical problem, if your brand's purchase or usage is driven by positive motives, advertising will be the best way to deal with brand attitude.

Beyond these general strategic implications, there are quite specific tactical considerations associated with each of the quadrants. While these are outside the scope of this book, it is important to know that the brand attitude quadrants will also direct your executions for both advertising and promotion.

To summarize, the Rossiter-Percy Grid helps with IMC planning in the following ways:

1. It helps focus your thinking about your product or service in terms of your target audience's involvement with the decision and the motivation that drives their behavior.

2. When involvement is low and motivation is negative, a wide variety of options are open because the target audience does not need to be "sold," only interested, and the key is in the information provided.

3. When involvement is high and motivation is negative, the target audience must be convinced by the message, so the communication options considered must be able to accomplish this.

4. When motives are positive, "emotional authenticity" is the key to successful communication, whether involvement is high or low, so the communication options considered must be able to deal with this.

Chapter Notes

[1] This is an important consideration, and one now being addressed by a number of research companies. For example, ARBOR Inc. has developed the notion of "core loyalty" to reflect not just what people may buy regularly, but also how strongly they are committed to that brand.

[2] J. R. Rossiter and L. Percy, *Advertising and Promotion Management* (New York: McGraw-Hill, 1987).

[3] Rossiter and Percy, *Advertising Communications and Promotion Management.*

[4] R. M. Prentice, "How to Split Your Marketing Funds between Advertising and Promotion Dollars," *Advertising Age*, January 10, 1977, 41–42; and "How to Reduce Tension, Improve Ad Productivity," *Advertising Age*, November 13, 1980, 71.

[5] Results of the 1994 POPAI study are discussed by Leah Havan in "Point of Purchase, Marketers Getting with the Program," *Advertising Age*, October 23, 1995.

[6] L. Percy and J. R. Rossiter, "A Model of Brand Awareness and Brand Attitude Advertising Strategies," *Psychology and Marketing* 9(4) (1992), 263–274; and Rossiter and Percy, *Advertising Communications and Promotion Management.*

[7] Ibid.; and J. R. Rossiter, L. Percy, and R. J. Donovan, "A Better Advertising Planning Grid," *Journal of Advertising Research* 31(5) (1991), 11–21.

[8] Rossiter, Percy, and Donovan, "A Better Advertising Planning Grid."

[9] J. C. Maloney, "Curiosity versus Disbelief in Advertising," *Journal of Advertising Research* 2(2) (1962), 2–8.

[10] The importance in processing marketing communication is often overlooked. While it can be difficult to identify the specific emotions that might best encourage processing a message, it is important to understand *how* emotion operates. John Rossiter and Larry Percy discuss this in a number of places, including: "Emotions and Motivations in Advertising," in R. H. Holman and M. R. Solomon (Eds.), *Advances in Consumer Research Vol. XVIII*, 1991; "The Role of Emotion in Processing Advertising," in M. Lynn and J. M. Jackson (Eds.), *Proceedings of the Society for Consumer Psychology*, 1991; and *Advertising Communications and Promotion Management.*

CHAPTER THREE

IMC Planning Tools

How does one go about making sense out of all the market information and communication options available when planning an integrated marketing communications program? Not only have brands, markets, and consumers become more complex in their behavior, but so too have the many varied (and growing) options of communicating with your target market. In days gone by, marketing communication seemed quite simple: run an ad if you wanted to talk with your consumer; run a promotion if you needed to achieve a specific, short-term tactical objective. This simple dichotomy no longer reflects the diversity of the communication process or the market.

We have emphasized that IMC is really about integrated planning of marketing communications options. In this chapter we introduce a series of planning tools that will help organize your thinking about the market you are addressing, relate appropriate marketing communication options to how your target market behaves, and generate creative briefs to guide the execution of your marketing communications.

IMC Planning Worksheets

Before we can begin to think of specific marketing communications, it is very important to carefully analyze what you know about your market. The first step is to outline the relevant market issues that are likely to affect your communications. Your best source of information will be the marketing plan, because all marketing communications efforts should be in support of the marketing plan. (If for some reason a marketing plan is not available, think seriously of developing one.[1] Otherwise, answer the questions posed in the Market Background Worksheet described below based upon the best available management judgment.) Next you will want to carefully consider your target market action objectives. Most markets have multiple target groups, and as a result, a number of communication objectives may be required to reach them. In fact, in today's world we generally need more than one level of communication, making IMC necessary. Finally, after looking at the market generally and your target market specifically, it will be time to think about overall marketing communication strategy. We shall now look into each of these three areas in some detail.

Marketing Background Worksheet

What is it about your brand, company, or service that might bear upon what you want to say to your target market? This may seem a simple question, but it really is not. Certainly you want people to know about all the good things you stand for, but this doesn't go far enough. While any marketer may have certain unique areas that will be important to address in an overview of their market background, there are at least six questions you will want to answer. (See Figure 3.1.)

Figure 3.1
Marketing Background Worksheet Questions

Key Consideration	Questions
Product Descriptions	What are you marketing?
Market Assessment	What is your overall assessment of the market where your product or service competes?
Source of Business	Where do you expect business to come from?
Competitive Evaluation	How does the competition position itself?
Marketing Objectives	What are the marketing objectives for your product or service?
Marketing Communication	How are marketing communications expected to contribute to the marketing objective?

Product Descriptions. What are you marketing? Write out a description of the product or service you are marketing so that someone totally unfamiliar with the product will understand what it is. This is really very important, because this information will serve as a background for the people who will be creating and executing your marketing communications.

Market Assessment. What is your overall assessment of the market where your product or service competes? This information must be current. If it comes from a marketing plan, be sure nothing has occurred that might "date" the information. What we are looking for here is knowledge about the market that is going to influence your success. Is the market growing, are there new entries, have there been recent innovations, bad publicity? While you need to provide enough information to communicate a good "feel" for the market, the description should be simple and highlight only the most relevant points.

Source of Business. Where do you expect business to come from? We need to look at this question in terms of both competition and the consumer. Again, this reflects the increasing complexity of today's markets. For example, who are the key competitors, and will your product or service compete with others outside the category? Where will customers or users of your product or service come from? What, if anything, will they be giving up? Will they be changing their behavior patterns? This is really the first step toward defining your target market (which is dealt with in detail in the next section), and begins to hint at how a better understanding of your target will lead to the most suitable communications options to reach them.

Competitive Evaluation. How does the competition position itself? What are the key claims made in the category? What are the creative strategies of the competition? What types of executional approaches and themes are being used? Here it is often helpful to append actual examples. Something else to include is an evaluation of the media tactics being used by competitors. What seems to be their mix of marketing communication options, and how do they use them? All of this provides a picture of the communications environment within which you will be competing.

Marketing Objectives. What are the marketing objectives for your product or service? This should include not only a general overview of the marketing objective, but specific share or financial goals as well. When available, the marketing plan will provide these figures. Otherwise, it is important to estimate the financial expectations for your product or service. If your marketing communications program is successful, what will happen? This is critical because it will provide a realistic idea of how many marketing dollars can reasonably be made available for the marketing communication program.

Marketing Communication. How is marketing communication expected to contribute to the marketing objective? As we now know from the previous chapter, the answer is much more than "increase sales." It is likely that marketing communication will be expected to make a number of contributions toward meeting the marketing objectives. This is where you will begin to get an idea of just how much will be expected from your marketing communication program, and the extent to which multiple messages and types of marketing communication might be required.

Target Audience Action Objectives Worksheet

Once we have thought through the market generally, it is time to focus more particularly upon whom we want to address with our marketing communications. When thinking about our target market we must look well beyond traditional demographic considerations. It is also important to think ahead. What type of person will be important to the future of our business? In this section of the IMC plan there are five questions to address. (See Figure 3.2.)

Where Are the Sales or Usage to Come From—Customers or Non-customers? While we always hope our business will be broadly based, realistically we must set a primary objective to reach customers or non-customers. Communication strategies will differ significantly depending upon which we choose, and even within these two categories, other distinctions can and should be made.[2] Are we interested primarily in loyal customers or those who use our product along with competitors'?

Figure 3.2
Key Target Audience Worksheet Questions

- Where are sales or usage to come from—customers or non-customers?

- Does the marketing objective involve initiating trial or continued usage?

- Where does the "trade" fit?

- What do we know about the target audience?

- Who are the decision makers the marketing communications must reach?

Promotional tactics would clearly differ between these two groups of customers. Among non-customers there are those loyal to someone else, those who switch among several but do not include us, and those who are not involved in the category at all. It is very important to think about various alternative market-relevant groups, and where it makes the most sense to place your primary communications effort.

Does the Marketing Objective Involve Initiating Trial or Continued Usage? In Chapter 2 we talked about trial and repeat purchase objectives. Which will be our primary objective? This may seem to be just another way of asking if we are talking to customers or non-customers. In many cases it will be, but not when marketing new products or line extensions. Some customers may use some of your products or services, but not others. But even when the question seems irrelevant, it is a good idea to think about it because it will remind you of the relationship between trial versus repeat objectives and where you expect your sales to come from.

Where Does the "Trade" Fit? It is important to think about the trade in the broadest possible terms, including all those who are involved in the distribution and sale of our product or service without necessarily buying or using it themselves. We will address where the trade might fit specifically in terms of how decisions are made in Question 5. What we need to think about here is whether or not people not directly concerned with the purchase and use of our product or service might nevertheless be an important part of the target audience for our marketing communications. For example, we may need to "pre-sell" a new product to distribution channels or inform possible sources of recommendations about our offer (for example, doctors or consultants).

What Do We Know about the Target Audience? Traditionally, target audiences have been described in demographic terms: "women, 18–34." Sometimes efforts have been made to include so-called "psychographic" or lifestyle descriptions. All of this is important, but it is not enough when we are considering integrated marketing communications programs. Now we must also understand our target audience(s) in terms of their behavioral and attitudinal patterns that are relevant to communication and media strategies. This means how they now behave or are likely to behave in relation to our product or service, what their differing information needs or motivations might be, and how they "use" various media.

Who Are the Decision Makers the Marketing Communications Must Reach? Here we must focus upon who all is involved in the decision to buy or use our product or service, and what roles they play in the decision process. As we noted in Chapter 2, people who study consumer behavior generally talk about five roles people play in the decision-making process (see Figure 3.3):

- An *initiator,* who proposes the purchase or usage

- An *influencer,* who recommends (or discourages) the purchase or usage

- The *decider,* who actually makes the choice

- The *purchaser,* who actually makes the purchase

- The *user,* who is the one to use the product or service

The importance of the role someone plays in the decision process for IMC cannot be emphasized enough. When we communicate with advertising or promotion we are talking to individuals, as *individuals in a role.* Our message must be consistent with that role. We want initiators to be aware of our product or service, and to be positively inclined to suggest its purchase or use. Influencers must be armed with arguments and given reasons to recommend our product or service. The decider must be persuaded to choose our product or service and the purchaser to actually make the purchase. Remember, the decider and purchaser may not be the same person, and there is always an opportunity for the purchaser to change his or her mind at the point of purchase. For users, we want to be sure not only that they do indeed use our product or service, but ideally that they do it quickly.

Decision Grid

As an aid to thinking about all who might be involved in the decision process and the roles they play, it is helpful to complete a Decision Grid (Figure 3.4). A Decision Grid is a simple but effective way of focusing your thinking about various roles members of your target audience are likely to play. For each of the five roles, imagine what members of your target audience (both consumer and trade) might fulfill that role in the decision to purchase or use your product or service. It is not necessary for the grid to be precise at this point. What we are trying to do is stimulate

Figure 3.3
Roles Target Audience Members May Play in the Decision Process

Role	Description
Initiator	Those who *propose* the purchase or usage of a product or service
Influencer	Those who *recommend* (or discourage) the purchase or usage of a product or service
Decider	Those who actually *make the choice* of what product or service to purchase or use
Purchaser	Those who actually *make the purchase* of the product or service
User	Those who actually *use* the product or service

our thinking about various target audience groups that might be important in the development of specific IMC recommendations. Later in this chapter we will be discussing a Behavioral Sequence Model, where we will use this preliminary thinking to develop a more specific and achievable model of our target audience's behavior.

To get an idea of how the Decision Grid can help organize and stimulate your thinking, let us consider some examples. In the simplest case, one individual is likely to play all of the roles involved, which would make

Figure 3.4
Decision Grid

	Target Audience	
Role	**Consumer**	**Trade**
Initiator		
Influencer		
Decider		
Purchaser		
User		

sense for something like laundry detergent or fabric softener. In this case we know that we have only one consumer target audience group to worry about. However, we must still be concerned about whether that person only requires a single message to stimulate purchase, or whether several messages, perhaps delivered in different ways, are necessary. Suppose we are marketing a new product to these individuals. In that case we will probably need more than one message, even though all the decision roles are played by the same person. For example, broadcast advertising does a great job of raising people's awareness and awakening latent interest in a product. Unfortunately, most packaged goods categories do not excite the consumer, so it is quite easy for people to forget about the new product. For that reason, it would make sense to provide an incentive for trial with a coupon, and an in-store display or shelf-talker to arrest the shoppers' attention and remind them of their interest in the product that the advertising generated. This, of course, will involve the trade as an influencer, and a need to include them in our planning.

If all we did was advertise, there would be no guarantee that the shopper would spot the item at the point of purchase because behavior in the store is so routinized. In this example, broadcast advertising would be great for driving up need, but additional help would be needed when the actual purchase decision is made—help advertising could not provide.

What if our new product is a children's cereal? Here we could imagine at least two different people involved in the decision process: a child as initiator, influencer, and user; and a parent as influencer, decider, and purchaser. Questions this might raise are: Do we need different advertising for child and parent to arouse interest in the product, or simply different media for delivery? Do we offer an incentive for trial to the child or parent, or is one even necessary (perhaps the interest of the child obviates the need for a trail incentive for either)? Would the parent be motivated enough by the child's influence to seek out the product at point of purchase during the actual purchase decision, or will an aid to recognition, such as a special display or shelf talker, be necessary? If so, we would again need to involve the trade.

In fact, we know that for any new product, marketing communications directed to the trade are essential. But when we are considering a Decision Grid, we are only interested in the role the trade might play in communicating directly with the consumer. Specific communications with the trade itself would require a separate Decision Grid.

Some decisions are much more involved than these examples. If we are marketing cruise vacations, for example, the decision whether or not to take a cruise, and if so with what cruise line, is much more involved than a simple packaged goods purchase. Figure 3.5 illustrates a possible Decision Grid for a cruise vacation. We know that deciding upon taking a cruise is no "snap" decision. Friends who have recently been on a cruise may be talking about it and encouraging the prospect to take one; family members who may or may not have taken a cruise could suggest the idea; or the prospect may think about it him- or herself. Marketing communications to any of these potential target groups could initiate the decision process. Travel agents (part of the trade) also could have a direct hand in initiating the decision process, for it is not unusual for them to suggest holiday opportunities to customers. Here is an example where the trade could play a role in directly communicating with the consumer during the decision process. All of these target groups might also play a role in influencing the decision.

Even if we went no further, we can see here a number of potential opportunities for communicating with target groups in various ways to effect a positive decision to take a holiday with a cruise line. For example, a discount on a future cruise for recent cruisers who recommend a friend, advertising directly to the potential cruiser, incentive programs to travel agents, and so on. The Decision Grid helps to open up this kind of thinking.

To finish our example, those most directly involved in paying for the cruise are most likely to assume the role of decider, and one of the deciders will most likely make the actual purchase. This purchase is much too

Figure 3.5
Decision Grid for a Cruise Vacation

	Target Audience for Cruise Vacation	
Role	**Consumer**	**Trade**
Initiator	Family member Friends who have been on a cruise Potential cruiser	Travel agent Cruise "fairs"
Influencer	Family member Friends who have been on a cruise Potential cruiser	Travel agent
Decider	Individual adult potential cruiser Adult couple potential cruiser	
Purchaser	Individual adult potential cruiser	
User	Adult cruisers	

highly involved to entrust the final details to anyone else. The users, of course, are all those likely to go on the cruise. Travel agents are unlikely to be involved as deciders, purchasers, or users.

You may have been wondering why we are concerned with the role of users. While a product is being used, especially when the usage experience is positive, is a perfect time to reinforce that positive experience. In our cruise example, while on board there would be any number of opportunities for reinforcing the choice the customer made. This can be especially important with high involvement decisions like this where there is a great deal of perceived risk in the decision (an automobile purchase is another good example).[3]

Communication Strategy Worksheet

In this section we are dealing broadly with overall communication objectives and strategy. Specific creative strategies for advertising, direct mail, point of purchase, and so on will be developed in the Creative Briefs that we prepare for specific communication tasks. We will be addressing the creative brief later in this chapter. In this section we will want to think about three questions (see Figure 3.6):

1. What are our communication objectives?

2. What is the brand attitude strategy?

3. What do we want people to do?

What Are Our Communication Objectives? In Chapter 2 we introduced five communication effects: category need, brand awareness, brand attitude, brand purchase intention, and purchase facilitation. We need to establish which of these possible effects of marketing communication are important to our overall communications strategy.

Figure 3.6
Key Communication Strategy Worksheet Questions

- What are our communication objectives?
- What is the brand attitude strategy?
- What do we want people to do as a result of our communications?

An important point to remember is that communication effects can be addressed by all forms of marketing communication. In other words, regardless of which type of marketing communication you are considering, it will have the ability to stimulate any of the major communication effects. However, as we have seen in Chapter 2, all types of marketing communication are not necessarily equally effective in creating particular effects.

Setting communication objectives is actually our first consideration of what we want our marketing communications to say about our product or service in order to cause the target audience to take the desired action (that is, positively fulfill their role in the decision process). Communication objectives are quite simply the communication *effects* we are looking for. Next, we will look at four of the five communication effects as they are likely to translate to objectives. Because purchase facilitation is a wide-ranging effect, it will not be considered here.

Category Need. If there is little demand for a category, or people seem less aware of it, establishing or reminding people of it becomes a communication objective. For example, one could not really do much of a job advertising or promoting a specific brand of a new product such as CD players until people learned just what they were. Market share leaders can also benefit from category need advertising. A not-too-long-ago example of reminding people of a category need was when Campbell Soup ran its "soup is good food" campaign. By stimulating category need for soup they generated differentially high sales for Campbell's because of their overwhelming share in the category.

Brand Awareness. Brand (including trade) awareness is *always* an objective of any marketing communications program, whether advertising or promotion. Remember, you must indicate whether this awareness will occur via recognition or recall. Recognition brand awareness is when the consumer sees the brand in the store and "remembers" it from the advertising or promotion. Recall brand awareness is when the consumer must remember the brand or store name first, prior to buying or using (for example, when a consumer decides to have lunch at a fast-food restaurant, or when an industrial buyer decides to call several suppliers for a quotation). A principal communication objective of all advertising is to create or maintain brand awareness.

While we think of brand awareness as a traditional strength of advertising, promotion can make an equally strong contribution. Generally, promotion is best utilized for increasing brand recognition. "Merchandised" promotions do this by drawing more attention to a brand at the point of purchase (for example, with coupons or special displays).

Brand Attitude. Brand attitude is *always* a communication objective. What we mean by brand attitude is the information or feeling we impart through our marketing communication. Information (benefits) or feeling (emotional associations) transmitted by consistent advertising over the long term can build "brand equity" where, again, the brand may be a store, product, or service.

Whereas we traditionally think of advertising for affecting brand attitude, the best promotions also work on brand attitude. These are what we call brand equity building promotions, as mentioned in Chapter 2. Usually the immediate aim of a promotion is a short-term increase in sales. However, a brand equity building promotion will also create more long-term communication effects, thereby maximizing full-value purchase once the promotion is withdrawn. For example, free trial periods or free samples help create a positive feeling for a brand, as do coupons as a small "gift" from the manufacturer. There are brand equity building promotions that provide useful information to ensure a continued favorable attitude after trial as well, such as regional training programs, cookbooks, on-package usage suggestions, and the like.

Brand Purchase Intention. Brand (or trade) purchase intention is a communication objective in which the primary thrust of the message is to "commit now" to buying the brand or using a service. Purchase-related behavioral intentions such as dealer visits, direct mail inquiries, and referrals are also included in this communication objective.

Along with brand awareness, stimulation of brand purchase intention is the real strength of promotion, as we shall see in Chapter 4. All promotions are aimed at moving sales forward immediately, and they do this by stimulating immediate brand purchase intentions, or other purchase-related intentions such as a visit to a showroom or a call for a sales demonstration. For consumer target audiences, the potential power of promotions is underscored by recent research that suggests purchase intention can be influenced at the point of purchase in about two out of every three supermarket decisions.[4]

What Is the Brand Attitude Strategy? We have noted that brand attitude (along with brand awareness) is always a communication objective. You will also recall from Chapter 2 that strategies for implementing the brand attitude objective are derived from one of the four quadrants of the Rossiter–Percy grid (Figure 2.9). Here you must decide which of the four brand attitude strategies apply:

- Low involvement/informational—this is the strategy for products or services that involve little or no risk, and where the underlying motivation for behavior in the category is one of the five negative motives. (You may want to look back at Figure 2.8 to refresh your memory of these motives.) Typical examples would include pain relievers, detergents, and routinely purchased industrial products.

- Low involvement/transformational—this is the strategy for products or services that involve little or no risk, but where the underlying motivation in the category is positive. Typical examples would include most food products, soft drinks, and beer.

- High involvement/informational—this is the strategy for products or services that involve risk (either in terms of price or for psychosocial reasons), and where the underlying behavior is negatively motivated. Typical examples would include financial investments, insurance, heavy duty household goods, and new industrial products.

- High involvement/transformational—this is the strategy for products or services that involve risk, and where the underlying behavior is positively motivated. Typical examples would include high fashion clothing or cosmetics, automobiles, and corporate image.

Once the general strategy has been selected, list the benefit claims you can make for the product or service that are related to the appropriate motives. For example, if you are marketing a new personal financial software system for home computers, this would likely require high involvement/informational brand attitude strategy. You would then want to list all the benefit claims you could make about this new system that will help satisfy the likely motive. For example, any of the negative motives (with the exception of normal depletion) might apply here, but we will assume our research has shown us that most people are not satisfied with existing personal finance software. This means behavior will be motivated by incomplete satisfaction. What is it about your system that addresses this motivation? These are the benefit claims you will want to think about. There may be other things you could say, but you only want to consider those things that are *directly related to the appropriate motive*.

What Do We Want People to Do? What *exactly* do we want people in our target groups to do after receiving our communications? Is there anything in particular they will need to do in order to respond to any specific aspect of our marketing communication in the way we want them to? For example, do we want them to call or visit for more information? Is what we want them to do something that they will need to think a lot about before acting or responding, or is it relatively easy? Is there anything we need to say or do to make responding easier for them?

The reason we need to think about this is that often there may be something about our product or service, its price, or its distribution that could make it difficult for people to respond to our marketing communications the way we want them to. This is what we talked about in Chapter 2 as *purchase facilitation*. If we do identify something in the marketing mix that could be a problem, purchase facilitation could become a communication objective. Advertising, for example, is sometimes called upon to try to ameliorate a problem until it can be rectified more concretely. For example, we suggested that if a new product becomes too successful and production has been overwhelmed, you might want to let people know and ask them to be patient. Advertising could also be used to draw attention to other benefits if there is a perceived weakness in the product or service, or try to justify a higher price (or even a lower price!), or try to turn limited distribution into a positive by saying "available only at selected outlets."

Promotion can really only have a moderate effect upon purchase facilitation; and usually at considerable cost. For example, with a severe price reduction a promotion can sometimes sell a poor product. Temporarily, a price promotion can help solve an overpricing problem. And a promotion can also help poor distribution by inducing customers to visit distant stores. Again, marketing problems can be lessened by promotion, but usually only temporarily.

Of course, in the end, if you really do have a serious problem, the problem must be solved. Marketing communications cannot sustain a troubled product or service indefinitely.

Developing a Behavioral Sequence Model

Introduced by Rossiter and Percy,[5] a Behavioral Sequence Model (BSM) is an invaluable planning tool for constructing an integrated marketing communications program. A BSM asks you to first think about the major *decision stages* members of your target audience utilize preceding, during, and following purchase or use of your product or service. Then for each of these major stages, it asks for the *decision roles* involved (those we identified for the Decision Grid), *where* that stage of the decision is likely to occur, the *timing* of the stage, and *how* it is likely to occur. What we end up with is a flow chart that identifies where members of the target audience are taking action or making decisions that will ultimately effect purchase.

While this may sound complicated, it really isn't. Based upon prior research or good marketer common sense and understanding of your market, a BSM is surprisingly easy to develop. The important thing is that you are beginning to think about where, in the buyer's decision process, marketing communications of some kind might be reasonably expected to influence the choice made.

Decision Stages

Two general forms of the BSM are shown in Figures 3.7 and 3.8. You will recall from our discussion of brand attitude strategies in Chapter 2 that we make a fundamental distinction between low and high involvement decisions. People who study consumer behavior see an important difference in how low versus high involvement decisions are made, and this difference is reflected in the two "generic" BSMs. In low involvement decisions, it is not necessary for the consumer to be convinced by a message because very little risk is attached to the outcome. As a result, once a need is aroused the decision to purchase or use is made almost immediately, with no need to look for more information or carefully evaluate the decision. This means that for a low involvement purchase decision, a three-stage BSM (Figure 3.7) should be adequate—need arousal followed by purchase and usage. On the other hand, because high involvement purchase decisions carry risk, buyers must be convinced they are making a good decision. This

Figure 3.7
Generic Behavioral Sequence Model for Low Involvement Product or Service Decisions

Consideration at Each Stage	Decision Stage		
	Need Arousal	**Purchase**	**Usage**
Decision roles involved			
Where stage is likely to occur			
Timing of stage			
How it is likely to occur			

Figure 3.8
Generic Behavioral Sequence Model for *High Involvement* Product or Service Decisions

	Decision Stage			
Consideration at Each Stage	**Need Arousal**	**Information Search and Evaluation**	**Purchase**	**Usage**
Decision roles involved				
Where stage is likely to occur				
Timing of stage				
How it is likely to occur				

means that once a need is aroused, there will be a need for information search and evaluation. So for high involvement purchase decisions, a four-stage BSM (Figure 3.8) is required—need arousal, then information search and evaluation, followed by purchase and usage.

While we have presented two general BSMs, the more you know about how your target audience makes purchase or usage decisions, the more specific your BSM can be. You should feel free to add, modify, or delete any part of the generic model that may not suit your particular product or usage decision pattern.

While the generic models are very useful, and can generally be adapted to almost any situation, always remember that the best model is the one that comes closest to how you know decisions are made in your category. For example, in many business situations, distribution or trade hurdles must be surmounted before there is any thought of need arousal in the target audience. Other decisions may be even more complicated; or quite simple. When you consider the appropriate decision stages for your product or service, they may be as descriptive as you like. The whole idea is to capture the essence of the decision process, and use this as the basis for planning.

Two examples should give you an idea of how this can be done. First, suppose you are a retailer that has a chain of lamp stores. Let us consider a hypothetical decision stage model for a lamp purchase, and compare it with our generic model. The first stage in the decision to buy a new lamp probably involves a decision to redecorate. One of the most popular ways to redecorate is to buy a new lamp. These two stages would constitute what we have called need arousal. Next, one must decide where to shop for the lamp, shop the store (or stores), and make a choice. These three steps would be part of what we have called information search and evaluation. Once the lamp has been chosen, the purchase is made and the lamp is taken home and used. The decisions stages would then be: decide to redecorate—consider new lamp—look for places to buy lamp—shop—select lamp—purchase—replace old lamp with new.

With the decision stages identified in this fashion, you proceed to construct a BSM in exactly the same way discussed for the generic model. It should be apparent just how helpful this discipline can be for IMC planning. Even with a simple example such as this retail store, you can see how thinking about the decision process suggests a number of possible ways to communicate with potential lamp purchasers. The most obvious insight here is that a lamp purchase is unlikely to take place outside the context of "redecorating" (and research has indeed suggested this). This means that to interest people in lamps you must first awaken an interest in "redecorating," or changing the look of a room.

As a second example, we will look at a business-to-business decision process. Suppose you manufacture commercial kitchen equipment that is distributed through restaurant supply companies. How does a restaurant supply company go about deciding what items and brands they will distribute? A probable decision model might begin with keeping an eye out for better stock in order to maintain a competitive edge. This would lead to an awareness of a potential new line or item to stock. These two stages would correspond to need arousal in the generic model. Once interest is aroused, the new item will then be compared with what is now carried: the information search and evaluation stage. If the evaluation is positive, the item will be ordered and added to their inventory: purchase. Once stocked, sales will be monitored, and if positive, the item or line will be reordered. These last two stages would correspond to our generic model's usage stage. The decision stages for a restaurant supply company then might be: monitor new items—identify potential items to carry—compare with current items stocked—if positive, add to stock—monitor sales—if good, reorder.

Again, the BSM would be completed based upon these decision stages, and the implications for IMC planning would be significant. In fact, here is a good example of where the decision process suggests it might make sense to pay a lot of attention to the usage stages. If indeed you are manufacturing a new kitchen product, how much end-user "pull" might be necessary to ensure sufficient sales for your customer, the restaurant supply company, to reorder? If initial sales might be expected to be slow, would it make sense to offer a reorder incentive? These are the kinds of questions a good BSM stimulates as you complete the IMC Task Grid discussed later.

Decision Roles

Once we have established the specific stages of the decision process, or selected one of the two generic BSMs, we must assign the roles individual members of the target audience are likely to play at each stage. We have already considered the roles important target audience groups are likely to play in the overall decision process when we completed the Decision Grid for the Target Audience Action Objective worksheet. Let's return to the Decision Grid for a cruise vacation, and see how this translates to the BSM.

Our first question, if we are going to use one of the two generic BSMs, is whether or not a cruise vacation is a low or high involvement decision. Clearly, it is a high involvement decision, where information search and evaluation will be necessary, so we need the high involvement BSM. What role is most likely to occur during the need arousal stage? Because those in the initiator role get the purchase process started, it is the initiators whom we want to include under *need arousal* in the model. From the Decision Grid we see that this would include family members, friends who have been on a cruise, potential cruisers, travel agents, and cruise "fairs."

Since influencers recommend and deciders choose what to do, both roles will be influential during the information search and evaluation stage of the decision process. The influencers included family members, friends who have been on a cruise, and travel agents. The decider is either an individual adult potential cruiser or a couple. The actual purchase is made by the purchaser, whom we identified as an individual adult potential cruiser, while the usage stage is experience by the user, whom we identified as an adult cruiser.

This may be a good point to deal with the issue of individual versus group decisions. It is certainly true that many family decisions are made through a husband/wife or family consensus, and many business purchase decision are the result of a group effort. However, when it comes to marketing communications, we are interested in the *individual* and the role he or she plays in the overall decision process. Our communication efforts must first persuade the individual prior to his or her participation in any group decision. So while many actual decisions are the result of group action, specific advertising or promotion must address individuals in the roles they are playing in the decision process.

Where Decision Stages Occur

Locating opportunities for marketing communication is vital to successful IMC, and a behavioral sequence model can help pinpoint likely places. In fact, as one considers a BSM, the first thing you notice is that different stages in the decision process occur at different times, and as a result where you can reach individuals as they play their roles at each stage can certainly vary. There are exceptions, of course. For example, the consumer might be shopping and someone gives him or her a sample of a new cookie to taste along with a coupon. The consumer likes it and decides to buy some. The cookies are in a special end-aisle display, so he or she picks up a box, opens it, and enjoys a few while finishing shopping. In this case all of the decision stages occur at one location—the store. However, this is not likely to be the case very often. And because potential locations can vary widely under different circumstances, unusual media services might be appropriate.

Looking again at our cruise vacation example, where is need arousal likely to occur? Some examples that come to mind for the customers would be at home or at a travel agency or visiting a cruise fair; and for travel agents or cruise fair operators, at their office. Remember, we are interested in travel agents and cruise fairs here as helping to initiate the decision process among potential customers, so communication designed for them would encourage their recommending our cruise line. Members of our consumer target groups, in their role as influencers or deciders, are likely to look for and evaluate information in the home, at a travel agency, at a cruise fair, or by talking with friends. Travel agents, in their role as influencers, will likely gather and evaluate information to play this role in their office, at trade shows, or on actual cruises. The deciders and purchasers are most likely to make the actual purchase decision at home or at the travel agency. Users will of course be on the cruise ship.

In the second edition of their book, Rossiter and Percy[6] build upon some recent work in the area of situations theory in buyer behavior and offer four points for marketing communications managers to consider for each location included in the BSM:

1. *How accessible is the location to marketing communication?* This could range from no accessibility to too much, in the sense of a lot of clutter from other marketing communications or competition from other things.

2. *How many role-players are present?* We need to know if our message is directed to an individual or if several people are participating in this stage of the decision at that location.

3. *How much time pressure exists?* This could range from none to a great deal and the greater the time pressure the less opportunity there will be to process the message. The difference between relaxing at home and dashing in and out of a store will seriously effect the likelihood of a message being processed.

4. *What is the physical and emotional state of the individual?* Certain personality states can seriously affect message processing. For example, is someone in a doctor's waiting room there for a routine check-up and generally relaxed (assuming they haven't been kept waiting too long) or because of symptoms of a serious illness and therefore upset and anxious?

As you can see, it is important to think about what is going on at each location where part of the decision is made. Some locations are going to be better than others as potential places to reach the target audience.

Timing of Decision Stages

The timing of decision stages should reflect the general purchase cycle or pattern for the category. Understanding when each stage of the decision process occurs and the relationship between the stages is important for media scheduling. Obvious examples would be seasonal decisions such as back-to-school shopping or holiday purchases. But understanding the timing of even such routine behavior as meal planning is important.

A good example of this is the decision process for choosing a dessert. Obviously, for the average day, what to buy and serve for dessert is a low involvement decision. In fact, most dessert decisions are made after the meal. This means that whatever is to be served must be on hand, and even more important, must be ready to serve. This is no problem for cookies, ice cream, and fruit, the most popular dessert choices. But what if you are selling cake mix or something like Jell-O? If all you do is sell the end product, all you will do is move the product from the store shelf to the pantry shelf. This does *not* move it from the pantry to the table. For a cake or Jell-O to be served for dessert it must have been made sometime before dinner. This suggests advertising to homemakers in the morning to make the dessert so it will be ready for dinner.

This example underscores the fact that even the simplest-seeming decision process can have hidden traps if you do not fully understand it. This is also why we talk about both purchase and usage in the decision stages.

Continuing with our cruise vacation example, when is need arousal likely to occur? Certainly when planning a holiday vacation, but perhaps at other times as well. For example, when thinking of a way to celebrate a special occasion such as a 25th wedding anniversary, the idea of a cruise might be a part of the thinking. And while such special occasion planning could occur at almost any time during the calendar year, would that also be true for holiday vacations? How far in advance do most people plan their annual holiday? As you can see, the BSM forces you to give careful consideration to questions that will have important implications for IMC planning. If you do not have the answers, you will need to decide if management judgment will do or if marketing research will be necessary.

Once the idea of a cruise vacation is seriously considered, information search and evaluation will take place over the next month or so. This means that information must be salient for both potential customers and travel agents during this period. This is the time when information on your cruise line must be easily available. The real question, as implied above, is just when in the calendar year is this likely to be concentrated, if at all: not all products are as predictable as those with clear purchase patterns like routinely purchased consumer products or seasonal products. The actual purchase is likely to occur immediately after the information gathered has been evaluated; and this is likely to be well in advance of the actual cruise. Given the very high involvement of this decision, this suggests that post-decision reinforcement (via, say, direct mail) might be a good idea. Finally usage, or the cruise itself, will follow.

How Decision Stages Occur

The last thing we want to consider in the BSM is *how* each of the stages are likely to occur. What is it that arouses need? How is the target audience likely to go about getting information? What are they likely to be doing at the point of purchase? In what way will the product or service be used? These are questions to ask in completing the generic BSM. If you developed a BSM tailored to the specific decision process associated with your product or service, you will want to ask similar questions for each stage: How is this likely to happen?

The usefulness of this for IMC planning is that it forces you to think about what is likely to be going on when various stages of a decision occur, and this will provide a perspective on marketing communication options that are likely to be effective under those circumstances. In our cruise example, need arousal will probably occur when members of the target audience are looking for something different or special to do on holiday. With normal vacation planning, a cruise is unlikely to be considered. Once considered, the target audience is likely to seek information in a variety of ways. They could talk with friends who have been on a cruise, visit a travel agent, call for brochures, or even visit a cruise fair if one happens to be in their area.

In fact, a casual interest in a cruise might initiate a visit to a cruise fair, which itself arouses more serious intent and information search and evaluation. Under these circumstances, the first two stages of the decision process could occur at more or less the same time. This would also be the case if someone visited a travel agent to talk about holiday options, and the travel agent suggested a cruise. The actual purchase stage is likely to occur with a phone call or visit to a travel agent. Usage, of course, occurs on the cruise.

Figure 3.9 illustrates how a BSM for the cruise vacation we have been discussing might look. It takes the generic model for a high involvement decision and summarizes what we know (or assume) about the decision process that is involved in choosing to take a cruise vacation. A completed BSM offers an overview of the kinds of information that are necessary if we are to design an effective integrated marketing communications program.

Figure 3.9
BSM for a Cruise Vacatiom

Consideration at Each Stage	Decision Stage			
	Need Arousal	**Information Search and Evaluation**	**Purchase**	**Usage**
Decision roles involved	Family members, friends who have been on a cruise, potential cruiser as initiator Travel agents and cruise fairs as initiator	Family members, friends who have been on a cruise, and potential cruiser as initiator Individual adult potential cruiser or couple as decider Travel agent as influencer	Individual adult potential cruiser as purchaser	All adults traveling on cruise as users
Where stage is likely to occur	At home, travel agent's office, or cruise fair for consumers At office for travel agent or cruise fair operator	At home, talking with friends, travel agent's office, or cruise fair for consumers At office, trade shows, or actual cruises for travel agents or cruise fair operators	At home or travel agent's office	On cruise
Timing of stage	Special trip or vacation holiday planning, or word of mouth	3–6 months following need arousal	Shortly after completing information search and evaluation	1–3 months after purchase
How it is likely to occur	Looking for something special	Ask, call, write for brochure, visit cruise fair, talk with experienced cruiser or travel agent	Call or visit travel agent	Enjoy cruise

The IMC Task Grid

Having answered the questions for the IMC planning worksheets and developed a BSM, we are at a point where we are now able to summarize the various communication tasks that will be required to satisfy our communication objectives. The worksheets have helped us set the strategic direction, and the BSM has alerted us to the many possible marketing communication options that might be required.

Together, the thinking that went into preparing these documents underscores the need for planning to occur at a central source. In addition to the logic of a single theme or "feel" for all of a brand's marketing communications, trade-offs must be made in the allocation of the communication tasks. Rarely do we have the resources to do everything we wish. These trade-offs are ideally centrally managed, and a BSM offers a good first look at what your options might be.

Utilizing the BSM, in conjunction with the target audience objective and communication strategy, you must decide whether or not your marketing communication program:

1. Can be satisfied with a single message directed at one primary target audience, using one primary type of marketing communication (e.g., advertising, direct mail, brochures, etc.) or

2. If a number of communication tasks should be considered, directed at one primary target, but to different roles in the decision process, different messages to different targets, and/or utilizing various types of marketing communications directed to different times or places in the decision process.

If the program objectives can be satisfied by a single message and type of marketing communication, you can proceed directly to developing a creative brief for that message (creative briefs are discussed in the last section of this chapter). If not, you should complete an IMC Task Grid, and then develop the appropriate creative briefs for the necessary communication tasks.

Communication Tasks

What are communication tasks? Simply put, it is what we want to happen as a result of our marketing communications. In technical terms, these are the five communication effects we introduced in Chapter 2. We looked at these possible effects in answering the questions for the Communication Strategy Worksheet, and determined those effects that are necessary to satisfy our strategic objectives. All we are doing at this point is summarizing them in practical terms for each stage of the decision process. In other words, we are beginning to draw together the thinking we have assembled into an overall IMC plan.

What communication effects are likely to be relevant to need arousal? Since this is the stage when someone begins to think about possible purchase or usage of a brand, there is no doubt brand awareness must be a primary objective. Brand attitude will also be involved, especially for low involvement decisions. It is clearly not enough for people to simply be aware of your product at this initial stage. Some positive attitude will also be required if you are to remain a contender in the decision process. But we must also consider category need here. It may not be necessary, but we should always ask ourselves if the target audience is both experienced and active in the category.

At the information search and evaluation stage we must be concerned with both brand attitude and brand purchase intention effects. Since the target audience must be both informed and convinced for high involvement decisions, it is essential that we provide the appropriate information at this stage. At the same time, especially when we are dealing with positive motives (which, incidentally, would be the case with our cruise vacation example), we must be nurturing the appropriate feelings as well. Authentically reflecting the emotion involved in such decision processes requires more than just a favorable attitude. We are also looking for a positive intention to buy or use our brand: brand purchase intention. As a result of a favorable evaluation of our brand, we want the target audience to choose it.

But the consumer's decision to choose our brand does not guarantee he or she will actually buy or use it. So at the actual purchase stage we want to ensure that the positive brand attitude is reinforced, and that the brand purchase intention is actually carried out. During usage, we want to continue to reinforce brand attitude and encourage repurchase or continued use of our brand. All of these decision stage–communication effects relationships in the generic BSMs are summarized in Figure 3.10.

Completing the IMC Task Grid

A generic IMC Task Grid is shown in Figure 3.11. As you can see, for each of the decision stages we must decide specifically which communication tasks we will be undertaking, whom in our target audience we will be

Figure 3.10
Decision Stage–Communication Effects Relationships

Decision Stage	Communication Effect
Need Arousal	Category Need, Brand Awareness, Brand Attitude (tentative)
Information Search and Evaluation	Brand Awareness, Brand Attitude, Brand Purchase Intention
Purchase	Brand Awareness, Brand Attitude, Brand Purchase Intention
Usage	Brand Attitude, Brand Purchase Intention

addressing at that stage, where and when we will be trying to reach them, and what marketing communication options we will be using. It is here that the overall IMC plan begins to take shape.

Communication Task. It is now time to translate the appropriate communication effect into a specific communication task. For example, we know we need brand awareness, but what kind (recall or recognition); and do we need to raise or simply maintain the awareness? With brand attitude, do we need to educate our target audience? Do we need to interest them, stimulate inquiry, give them a good feeling, or underscore a unique feature? Do we want brand purchase intention to mean a commitment to call and make a reservation or place an order, or to ask for more information? Should the target audience request our product specifically from an investment broker or health-care provider, or do we want them to pick up our brand on their next visit to the store?

What we want here is a clear, concise interpretation of the communication effects required to meet our overall objectives.

Audience. What specific members of our target audience are we seeking to address at each stage? The information will come from the BSM. However, it would be rare indeed that all of the potential target audience members in all of their roles would be included. This is where we must begin making choices. Which target audience members in what roles are critical? These become our primary target audiences. You may wish to identify secondary or even tertiary audiences, and see if they will be affordable. But what we are aiming for with the IMC Task Grid is to use the results of our thinking-through of all the potential routes to maximize our marketing efforts through marketing communications by using the *best* routes.

Where and When. From the BSM we will be looking for the best ways of reaching our target audience. Again, our worksheets and the BSM will have given us an opportunity to consider a wide range of likely places to access the target audience while they are engaged in the decision process. But now we must select those we feel offer the absolute best potential, singly or in combination.

IMC Options. This is where we specify exactly how we expect to communicate with the target audience to satisfy each communication task. How are we going to sustain recognition awareness? Should we use print advertising, billboards, or coupons? Will we use broadcast advertising or direct mail to educate our target audience? To facilitate purchase, do we want in-store banners or special displays? What about incentive promotions? (Chapter 5 will go into some detail describing various promotion options.)

Once we have completed the IMC Task Grid, we will have in effect laid out a plan for an integrated marketing communications program. While it is quite possible that the IMC plan ends up utilizing only advertising or only direct mail or some other promotional program, this does not alter the fact that it was an *integrated* marketing communications plan. Why? Because the planning process allowed for any and all marketing communication options to be considered, and this is what IMC is all about. We did

Figure 3.11
IMC Task Grid

Decision Stage	Communication Task	Target Audience	Where and When	IMC Options
From Decision Grid list appropriate decision stages	List *specific* result desired from the appropriate communication effect needed at each stage	Determine primary target audience group to reach at each stage	Determine best way of reaching primary target audience group at each stage	List best IMC option for satisfying each communication task

not enter the planning process with preconceived ideas (or at least we should not). We were not looking for an advertising or a promotion solution, we were looking for the *best* solution.

Completing an IMC Task Grid gives us an opportunity to pull together everything we know about what we want to do with our marketing communications. This permits us to objectively review what we know and look for the marketing communication solutions that best fit our needs and budget.

But this does *not* mean that the IMC Task Grid (Figure 3.11) provides the "answer." What it provides is a summary of your best reading of everything you know, and what you hope to accomplish with your marketing communications program. If you had all the money you needed, you could in fact proceed directly to implementing everything outlined in the IMC Task Grid. Unfortunately, that is rarely the case. Realistic budget constraints will no doubt limit what you may like to accomplish. But using the IMC Task Grid as a guide, it will be possible to make more efficient and effective decisions on which communication tasks to implement.

The Creative Brief

You may be wondering why we are including a discussion of the creative brief in a chapter on IMC planning tools. Creative briefs are a common tool in advertising planning, but much rarer in promotion planning. The reason we must deal with them here is that creative briefs are useful for the creation of *all* marketing communications, and in the case of IMC *must be congruent.*

As we shall see in the next chapter, at a macro level either advertising or promotion will form the primary thrust of an IMC program. Which one predominates is determined using the IMC Task Grid. In this section we will merely outline what goes into a creative brief. In Chapter 4 we will look at how creative briefs must be considered within the context of an overall IMC program.

The creative brief format outlined in this section includes all of the points that are essential to an effective creative execution. Many companies and advertising agencies have their own ways of writing a creative brief, but most will in some fashion or other cover the ten key areas discussed here. Overall, we might think of a creative brief in three sections: one that helps us define the task at hand, one that is principally concerned with the creative objectives, and one that is concerned with executional elements.

Task Definition. The first four points of our creative brief outline deal with task definition: *key market observation, source of business, customer barrier/insight,* and *target audience.* The purpose of these points is to help answer why we are putting this marketing communications program together. What are we hoping to do, whom are we talking to with this creative, what do they already know, think, or feel about us and our product or service, what are we trying to effect? All of this information will be available from your Marketing Background and Target Audience Action Objectives Worksheets. The four points that help define the specific task are:

1. Key market observation—what one point can you make about the market that will help the creatives understand and believe in the rest of the brief? There is no need to be exhaustive, just provide the basics.

2. Source of business—where, specifically, do we expect our business to come from? We are not looking for general descriptions here, but specific sources (e.g., current holders of long-term CDs, people unhappy with the performance of their current product, etc.).

3. Consumer barrier/insight—what one thing do we know about our potential target market that we may need to overcome, or that may help us reach them? What do they know, or think they know, about the product or product category; how do they feel about it; how interested are they in it; how do they distinguish between different products?

4. Target market—what is the most vivid description we can offer of the types of individuals to whom this communication will be directed? This description must go further than a simple listing of demographics or even lifestyle characteristics. We will want to provide enough information for the creatives to be able to picture in their mind's eye whom they are addressing.

Objectives and Strategy. The next four points deal with communication objectives and strategy. What we are seeking to do is help provide creatives with the best orientation possible, including the *one point* that, if communicated, will achieve our desired objective. Also, we are providing the evidence we have to convince our target audience.

1. *Communication objectives and tasks*—what is the specific communication objective for this creative, and where does it fit within the total IMC program? Here is where we designate the primary objective (category need, brand awareness, brand attitude, brand purchase intention, purchase facilitation) from the Task Grid and what communication task we hope to accomplish.

2. *Brand attitude strategy*—what do we know about the way customers make decisions? Here is where we lay out whether the decision is high or low involvement, and whether behavior is positively or negatively motivated. This positions the strategy into one of the four strategic quadrants.

3. *Benefit claim*—what is the *primary* consumer benefit and why? Here is where we identify the benefit claim that is most strongly associated with the relevant motivation, and provide the evidence that supports our choice. Anything that could be used in the communications to demonstrate or communicate the correctness of the benefit claim should be included. For example, if we understand customer motivation to likely center upon incomplete satisfaction, pointing out comparative advantages and how we should present them might be appropriate.

4. *Desired consumer response*—what is it that we want the target audience to know, think, feel, or do as a result of the communication? This should be a brief summary of what we expect to happen.

Execution. The last two points in the creative brief deal with the actual execution, providing guidance on what sort of communication this should be, what information must be included, and how we hope the target audience will respond to the execution. Those last two points are:

1. *Creative guidelines*—what tactics are appropriate for the type of brand awareness involved, and for the strategic quadrant chosen?

2. *Requirements/mandatory content*—what are the requirements, either creatively, legally, or corporately, that must be included? Here, for example, is where the logo treatment is spelled out.

Now that we have detailed each of these points, there is one thing to always keep in mind when putting together a creative brief. It is important to create a balance between including enough information for clear guidance and providing so much information that the creative people working on the assignment are placed in the position of working out their own communication priorities from the information provided. Generally speaking, there are two areas where it is hard to give too much information—target market and support for the benefit claim. But for the rest, keep it to the bare essentials. The creative brief should be complete on one page (an example is shown in Figure 3.12). All of this information comes from the worksheets and IMC Task Grid, and if more detail is desired, creatives should be referred to those documents.

Figure 3.12
Creative Brief Outline

Product	Job	Date
Key Market Observations		
Source of Business		
Consumer Insight		
Target Market		
Communication Objectives and Tasks		
Brand Attitude Stratetgy		
Benefit Claim and Support		
Desired Consumer Response		
Creative Guidelines		
Requirements/Mandatory Content		

Chapter Notes

[1] Almost any good marketing management text will discuss and provide examples of a marketing plan, for example any edition of Philip Kotler's *Marketing Management* (Englewood Cliffs, NJ: Prentice-Hall, Inc.). More detailed discussions can be found in marketing strategy texts such as any edition of D. J. Luck and O. C. Ferrell, *Marketing Strategy and Plans* (Englewood Cliffs, NJ: Prentice-Hall, Inc.).

[2] Rossiter and Percy, *Advertising Communications and Promotion Management.*

[3] When there is a high level of risk involved with a decision, once the decision is made there is an effort to justify that decision. For example, once someone purchases an automobile, it is not unusual for them to pay particular attention to advertising and other marketing communications to reinforce the choice they made. This is something psychologists call *reducing cognitive dissonance.* The psychologist perhaps most associated with this notion is Festinger. See, for example, L. Festinger, *Conflict, Decision and Dissonance* (Stanford, CA: Stanford University Press, 1964).

[4] K. Shermach, "Study: Most Shoppers Notice P-O-P Material," *Marketing News*, January 2, 1995.

[5] Rossiter and Percy, *Advertising Communications and Promotion Management.*

[6] Ibid.

Integrating Advertising and Promotion

In Chapter 2 we discussed how both traditional advertising and promotion work on the same five communication effects, and later we said how any (or all) of these communication effects can become objectives for a marketing communications program. In this chapter we will be looking at how we can optimize the strengths of advertising and promotion for an effective IMC campaign. In a sense, we can think of our job as implementing an IMC program by instilling the appropriate basic communication effects into the minds of our target audience. How we go about the job is by selecting the best combination of marketing communication options to achieve these effects.

In general, the relative communication strengths of advertising and promotion were shown in Figure 2.1. We saw that traditional advertising generally makes its strongest contributions to brand awareness and brand attitude, while promotion generally makes its strongest contributions to brand awareness and brand purchase intention. But to continue to emphasize a point we made earlier, the best promotions are those that *also* work on brand attitude (they help reinforce brand equity).

Promotion and advertising both work through communication, and either one can perform all the communication tasks. In IMC planning, our job is to find the best communications mix to reach our overall communication objectives and the best means of delivering our message to our target audience at the least overall cost.

Beyond the different overall strengths of advertising and promotion as they relate to communication objectives that we discussed in Chapter 2, a number of other marketing factors affect the relative effectiveness of advertising versus promotion, whether we are addressing a consumer, business, or trade target audience. These strengths are discussed in the section below.

Market Characteristics That Determine the Relative Effectiveness of Advertising Versus Promotion

In a very interesting study, senior marketing executives from large companies that manufacture nondurable consumer goods were interviewed.[1] Among other things, they were asked whether they felt different market scenarios would be likely to increase the importance of either advertising over promotion, promotion over advertising, or have no effect. While we must bear in mind that these are basically packaged goods marketers, the results nevertheless provide valuable insight into how marketers actually allocate their marketing dollars in communication planning.

One of the points made by the study, for example, is that marketers feel that advertising is more important than promotion earlier in a product's life cycle (especially in the so-called "growth" stage), and that promotion is more important late in the product's life (especially in the decline stage). This, of course, fits nicely with our understanding of the overall strategy of advertising versus promotion just mentioned. It is essential to build and nurture brand equity as a product grows, and this is what brand attitude, advertising's strength, is all about. A product in decline is often being phased out, and while we want product to move through the pipeline, we are not interested in any real investment in the brand. The tactical strength of promotion to stimulate brand purchase intention fits this need well.

Four categories of market characteristics culled from the study that seem to call for different advertising versus promotion strategy are discussed in the following sections. In each case our understanding of the relative effectiveness of advertising versus promotion is echoed by the marketing executives interviewed.

Product Differentiation

If your product or service is truly different from competition in the mind of your target audience, and that difference is seen as meaningful, you have a strong reason to advertise that difference. On the other hand, if the target audience perceives everyone in the category as more or less the same, in the short term promotion will make more sense than advertising. In the long term we would hope to create a meaningful perceptual if not actual difference for our brand. In fact, we must remember that when we talk about differentiated brands, we are talking about *perceived* differences. Whether or not the difference is "real" is beside the point if the target audience believes it is real.

Two general characteristics we should consider are price and quality. In both cases, when consumers perceive a difference, it calls for attention to how we use advertising and promotion. If your product or service is seen as significantly higher in price than other major competitors, advertising is more important than promotion. At first this may seem counter-intuitive, but upon reflection you will see that it really isn't. Yes, a price promotion will make a higher-priced brand *temporarily* more price-competitive, but it does nothing to justify the brand's regular price. Advertising, via brand attitude, can build brand equity and provide a reason why a higher price is justified.

Once again we must be alert to perceptions. For example, consumers "know" that Stouffer's frozen prepared side dishes are priced higher than either Bird's Eye or Green Giant. But is the difference really significant? Interestingly, the actual price is not that much higher (often all but comparable, or no more than a few pennies more), but the *perception* is that it is much higher. Under such circumstances it makes no sense to decry this misconception of a significantly higher price, and to try to convince people that for only a little more you get a much better product. Consumers believe it is better, so advertising must reinforce this perception along the lines of "naturally it costs more—good quality is expensive."

If you are seen as offering higher quality than your major competitor, it makes sense to advertise and reinforce this equity. If you in fact offer a lower-quality product or service than your major competitors, promotions will often help overcome a reluctance on the part of the target audience to "trade down."

In general we can say that when your product or service is perceived to be positioned differently from major competitors, advertising is more important than promotion in your IMC planning.

Market Position

If your product or service is frequently purchased or used, advertising is more important in the marketing communication mix than promotion. There are many reasons for this, but again they center around the need to continually reinforce a positive brand attitude under circumstances where the opportunity for brand switching is high. Promotions may of course be used tactically, but without a strong brand equity all promotions really do is "steal" usage. This is a problem underscored by the "cola wars" of the mid 1990s. Both Coke and Pepsi seem to have abandoned a consistent, unique advertising campaign that nurtures their brand equity, and turned more and more to price promotion. As a result, it is not unusual for the leading brand in a market at any one time to be the one with the best promotion. If taken to an extreme, this can lead to brand suicide.

It also makes more sense to advertise than to use extensive promotion when you have a clear market share advantage. Once again, it is the brand attitude strength of advertising that nurtures the brand equity that sustains market share advantage.

Overall then, with a strong market position through either frequent purchase or high market share advantage, advertising will be more important than promotion in your IMC planning.

Poor Performance

When a brand finds itself struggling, promotion becomes more important than advertising. When what is needed is help *now*, the more immediate sales results from promotion make sense. This flows naturally from promotion's strength, brand purchase intention. We must remember that this is unlikely to provide a long-term solution to the problem, but it is definitely a way to accelerate sales in the short run. This in turn should help increase cash flow and a return to the marketing plan.

A corollary to this is when you are in danger of losing distribution (which can be a natural consequence of disappointing sales performance) or having trouble building distribution. This is a perfect time to use trade promotion.

So when brand performance, either at the store or trade level, is faltering or not up to expectation, promotion will assume more importance than advertising in your IMC planning.

Competitive Activity

Not surprisingly, when competitors cut advertising and increase promotion, most brands will follow suit for fear of losing sales. If competitors increase spending on advertising while cutting back on promotion, again most brands will do the same. While this may make sense as a short-term tactical move, the actions of competitors should not necessarily guide your own marketing communication strategy. Each brand must take a careful look at its own situation, and respond in its own best interest.

As we noted above, a high-priced brand may indeed increase its advertising expenditures (correctly) to help nurture a strong positive attitude toward the brand in the face of aggressive pricing strategies by competitors. But if you are a "price" brand, not only should you probably not increase your advertising expenditures, you may wish to counter with even deeper short-run price promotions. The point here is that each situation must be looked at within the context of your own marketing objectives and your position in relationship to major competitors.

In recent years, at least for consumer packaged goods, there has been a strong increase in market share for private label products. Private label remains a small proportion of any market, but its share can certainly rival the share of many individual brands in a category. Where private label is a significant factor, it makes sense to increase advertising activity, not try to compete on price with promotion. More often than not this will take the form of stressing quality or some other aspect of brand equity.

Unfortunately, as Neilson statistics and IRI scanning data continue to show, as shares increase for private label brands too often companies turn to price promotions rather than attempting to reinforce the equity value in their brand. One recent exception to this, however, was Kraft's decision to cut margins significantly, but not at the expense of advertising, in order to recapture the macaroni and cheese market from store brands.

What we are talking about here are traditional private label brands, not the new "branded" private label products such as President's Choice. These better-quality private label products (in fact often of comparable quality with national brands) must be considered just like any other lower-priced competitor. The actual price differences are generally not that great, and they are being marketed much like any other widely distributed brand.

So, how do we treat competitive activity in IMC planning? We must look at each situation and respond with increased advertising or promotion in the best interest of our brand regardless of what major competitors may be doing. This usually means a short-term tactical response, increasing advertising or promotion when competitors increase theirs, but this need not be a blind response. Also, when private label is a serious competitor, increased emphasis on advertising is usually called for.

Overall, we have seen that various market conditions will direct our strategic and tactical uses of advertising and promotion. We cannot afford to think of advertising and promotion as independent means of marketing communication. Each has particular strengths, and within each there are particular types of advertising or promotion that may be used singly or in combination to address various situations in the market. It is not a question of "should we use advertising or promotion," but rather "should we *emphasize* advertising or promotion" in our IMC planning. The market considerations discussed and their impact upon IMC planning are summarized in Figure 4.1.

Figure 4.1

Impact of Market Characteristics upon Advertising vs. Promotion Emphasis in IMC Planning

MARKET CHARACTERISTIC	IMC PLANNING EMPHASIS
Product Differentiation:	
Positively perceived difference	Advertising emphasis
Market Position:	
High share	Advertising emphasis
Frequently purchased	Advertising emphasis
Poor Performance:	
Slow sales	Promotion emphasis
Distribution problem	Promotion emphasis (trade)
Competitive Activity:	
Competition increases advertising or promotion	Assess situation carefully and respond accordingly
Strong private label	Advertising emphasis

The Advantages of Using Advertising and Promotion Together

We have noted that more money is spent today in marketing communications areas outside of traditional advertising. In fact, the ratio is about three to one. However, for most marketing communications problems, traditional advertising will almost always be central to your marketing communications planning.

What is it about using advertising and promotion together that offers advantages relative to using only advertising or promotion? We have already discussed the fact that advertising and promotion have different strengths in relation to communication objectives. But the critical communication objective with regard to the joint effectiveness of advertising and promotion is advertising's prior establishment of a strong brand attitude, which is the main link to brand equity.

Don Shultz, while perhaps not going quite so far as this, when he talks about the role traditional advertising has to play in IMC,[2] does state that "image advertising is a critical ingredient in any marketing and communications program." He goes on to talk about the need to "protect or build the perceptual value of the brand." To our way of thinking, this is just another way of talking about brand equity, and the communication strength of advertising, brand attitude. We may approach the matter somewhat differently, and use different words, but there is no doubt that advertising must almost always play a crucial role in IMC planning.

The key to this importance lies in the fact that when advertising has been effective in generating a strong brand attitude that has led to a strong brand equity, all of your promotional efforts will be that much more effective. There are two fundamental reasons for this:

- First of all, when your target audience holds strong favorable attitudes toward your brand, it means that when you do use promotions the target audience will see them as a much better value, and

- When your target audience holds strong favorable attitudes toward your brand, when competitors offer promotions the target audience will be less likely to respond to them.

If you think about it, this makes sense. The more consumers like a product or service, the less likely they will be to switch because of promotion; and when the brand offers its own promotion, they will think just that much better of it, *and* it will tend to reinforce their already positive brand attitude.

Now, before we leave the impression that advertising, in creating a favorable brand attitude, may be all you really need, there is something else to consider. No matter how favorable your brand attitude, it is unlikely that everyone in your market buys or uses your product exclusively. In fact, it is unlikely that your core market is even dominated by totally brand loyal customers. What brand attitude is working on is maintaining a dominant share of favorable brand switchers. Of course it also holds brand loyal customers, but in today's markets consumers switch among various competitive alternatives. Unfortunately, this phenomenon of declining loyalty is being accelerated by an over-reliance upon promotion, especially price promotion, to attract switchers. We have already referred to the cola wars. In fact, in one major supermarket chain in New York state, over 80 percent of all Coke and Pepsi sales are as a price-off deal. The leading brand is simply the brand on special that day.

This does not change anything we have just discussed about the critical importance of advertising; it only underscores the fact that it is advertising and promotion working together that will create the most effective IMC programs.

Without effective advertising, it is unlikely that you will maintain brand equity over time. But, this must be coupled with appropriate use of promotion. We can best see how this strategy of combining advertising and promotion optimizes IMC planning by looking at something marketing consultant Bill Moran has called the "ratchet effect."[3]

The Advertising and Promotion "Ratchet Effect"

The notion of a "ratchet effect" rests upon the ideas we have just been talking about. When advertising is used in combination with promotion, it increases the value of your promotions while minimizing the effect of competitor promotion.

As we mentioned earlier, promotions tend to "steal" sales, especially from existing customers. The promotion more often than not will merely accelerate an already planned purchase by customers, or attract a switcher to your brand for this purchase only. The hope, of course, is that the promotion will increase the number of purchases of your brand by switchers. In other words, encourage them to "switch-to-us" more often. But without advertising support, what reason would there be? If someone is using (for example) coupons as the key to switching, *without* a coupon or other price promotion, your brand's likelihood of selection will not be good.

As a result, when you run a promotion, it should generate higher-than-normal levels of sales. But with promotion alone, without adequate prior advertising, once the promotion is over sales levels will dip below average levels until the product purchased on promotion has been exhausted, and customers are back in the market—that is, switchers are back on their normal switching pattern and loyal customers have used up the product they stocked up on while it was on promotion. This effect is illustrated in Figure 4.2

However, when advertising and promotion are used effectively together, the effect of promotion on top of prior advertising is to increase the rate of growth stimulated by advertising alone. Remember, of course, that this rate of growth may be flat or even declining. There is no guarantee that advertising alone will stimulate sales growth. The point is that the combination of advertising and promotion should improve overall market performance when it is part of a good IMC program.

This is what Moran has described as the "ratchet effect."[3] Because of prior advertising, there is a positive brand attitude. When the brand is promoted, loyal customers' favorable brand attitude is reinforced.

Figure 4.2
Effect of Promotion without Advertising

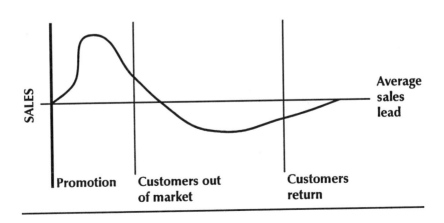

Switchers, attracted by the promotion, will be more likely to continue purchasing or using the brand on a more regular basis after the promotion is withdrawn because of the advertising's positive brand attitude effect. This means the regular customer base grows, and the average sales level "ratchets" up. This "ratchet effect" is illustrated in Figure 4.3.

All of this assumes, of course, that the combination of advertising and promotion is cost effective and the IMC campaign has been well conceived and truly integrated. We must be alert to the fact that price promotion has the potential of actually increasing prices at the consumer level. As marketing consultant Chuck Middelstadt points out, there are major costs tied to promotions, beyond the obvious. Uneven production runs and distribution adds cost. Carrying extra inventory costs the trade money. Tracking promotions can absorb a great deal of brand marketing overhead. In-store pricing and repricing adds costs. Without careful planning, all of this could lead eventually to significant price differentials.

The Impact of Demand Elasticity

At the heart of consumer response to this interaction between advertising and promotion is the economist's notion of *demand elasticity*. Again, this is a point made by Moran. Understanding the relationship between our brand's and competing brands' demand elasticities is an

---

Figure 4.3
Effect of Promotion with Advertising

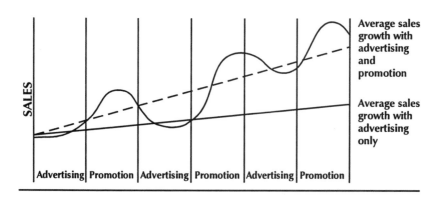

SALES

| Advertising | Promotion | Advertising | Promotion | Advertising | Promotion |

Average sales growth with advertising and promotion

Average sales growth with advertising only

---

important part of IMC planning. Specifically, in Moran's terms, we need to be concerned with "upside" and "downside" elasticities. We especially like his ideas here because they focus our thinking on the relationship between advertising and promotion in affecting sales, not simply the overall price elasticity of a brand.

As you might guess, "upside" elasticity refers to the sales increases resulting from a price cut or promotion; "downside" elasticity refers to the sales decline resulting from a price increase. While these definitions reflect our action with regard to pricing strategy, it is important to understand that our *competitors'* pricing strategy will directly affect the demand elasticity of our brand—both "upside" and "downside." Competitors' price increases in effect "cut" our price, just as aggressive price cutting or promotion by competitors in effect "raises" our price.

The ongoing market dynamic, especially in a time of heavy price-oriented promotion, underscores the need for effective advertising in most IMC programs. Our discussion of positive brand attitude and brand equity illustrates how effective prior advertising creates a more fertile ground for long-term sales benefit from promotion. We also discussed how effective prior advertising helps lessen the impact of competitor promotion. In other words, relative to competitors, effective advertising will generate high "upside" elasticity and low "downside" elasticity.

Your brand's "upside" and "downside" elasticities will depend to a great deal on its current brand equity (unfortunately, an elusive concept to measure). As a result, to the extent that your promotional activities contribute to brand attitude and reinforce brand equity, they will make advertising's job easier. Brand equity oriented promotions act just like advertising, increasing "upside" demand elasticity and reducing "downside" demand elasticity. As a result, with the exception of short-term tactical promotion, all of your IMC should aim for positive demand elasticity.

We are not suggesting that a firmly calibrated calculation of demand elasticities must be a part of IMC planning, only that it is important to think about it. We know, for example, that frequent or heavy price promotion on its own can negatively affect brand attitude. Many observers feel this is exactly what happened to Sears. In the early 1990s, Sears was a company in real trouble, and much of that trouble could be attributed to almost continuous price-cut promotion. Whether the heavy new advertising campaign of the mid 1990s will save the company remains to be seen. At least they are now using advertising to build a positive brand attitude in combination with their price promotions.

Think about where you stand in terms of your target audience's brand attitude toward you and your major competitors, what your pricing strategy is compared to competition, and how you are allocating your marketing dollars compared to competitors. This, along with the preceding discussion, should greatly help your understanding of the interdependence of advertising and promotion in successful IMC planning.

Advertising and Promotion Consistency

As we are planning IMC programs, it is essential to keep in mind the need for consistency of communication objectives for everything that is done for a brand. If we are trying to grow the category, then advertising and promotion must both work toward this end. This is also true if we are trying to increase brand awareness or stimulate immediate purchase intentions. Most important of all, it is vital to maintain consistency in marketing communications when addressing the brand's attitudinal positioning or "image," your equity with customers. While advertising can create this image, all other forms of marketing communication must support it.

This leads to one of the most critical considerations in IMC planning, the need for a consistent look or "feel" to all of your marketing communications. It is really surprising how many marketers do not seem to understand this. Too often, if you compare the advertising and promotion for a brand there is almost nothing in common (with the exception of the name, of course). This does *not* mean that every execution must be the same. In fact, some variation in execution is essential to maintain attention and interest, and to help forestall wearout. What we need is a unique look or feel to everything that is done so that the target audience recognizes your marketing communications as yours, even before they see the name.

Why Consistency Is Important

When we introduced communication effects back in Chapter 2, we pointed out that two of them are always communication objectives: brand awareness and brand attitude. Regardless of whether we are using direct mail, telemarketing, point-of-purchase merchandising, or traditional advertising, all of our marketing communications must be united in linking a common "image" with the brand name. While individual messages may (and should) vary, the underlying theme must remain the same. The key to this underlying theme will almost always be visual.

What we want to happen is for people to associate with our name a visual "sense" or cue that reflects the image of our product or service, and our name with the appropriate category need. If all of your marketing communication projects that visual cue, your target audience will associate it with your brand. This synergy builds overall positive response to everything you do. An advertisement recalls a direct mail package; in-store merchandising recalls an ad or mailing. You don't start from scratch with each piece of marketing communication, trying to effect a positive brand attitude.

The Visual Look Must Be Unique

The very reasons for a consistent look among all of your various pieces of marketing communication argue for its uniqueness. If there is any chance that the target audience may confuse your marketing communications with someone else's, the problem is obvious. Yet there is an incredible amount of similarity between marketing competitors' communications. One is reminded of the experiment conducted a few years ago by some academic researchers who switched the audio tracks from the commercials for two major soft drinks, and there was almost no distortion in the resulting commercials. The choreography from each of the two commercials was not out-of-sync with the competitor's sound track! In effect this was one commercial for two brands.

While this is an extreme example, pick up any newspaper or magazine and look at how similar much of the advertising for competing brands looks. This is especially true of retail store advertising, bank advertising, and automotive advertising.

What we want are unique executions that all have the same look or "feel," and that are firmly associated with our brand. Every piece of marketing communication, from packaging to promotion to advertising, should project the same image for our product or service. Good IMC planning helps ensure this.

Consistent Creative Briefs

Without IMC planning, it is almost impossible to have consistent creative briefs for various types of marketing communication. It is difficult enough when there is effective IMC planning. The problem, of course, is that there are usually different vendors involved: an advertising agency, direct mail or merchandising specialists, sales promotion agencies, and so on. Compounding the problem, often there are different people within a marketing organization assigned to deal with different vendors. The likelihood of them all getting together on their own to ensure a consistent output is slight.

Yet we have just seen how important it is that everything in a marketing communication campaign have a common look or "feel." Making sure this happens is one of the real strengths of effective IMC planning. It is not easy (an issue we will address fully in Chapter 9). The first question one must ask is: what is the *primary* communication option for this campaign? The answer comes from the IMC Task Grid. We are primarily interested in whether a message-oriented or a promotion-oriented program will drive the campaign. In other words, will most of our marketing dollars be directed toward a message-oriented advertising or direct mail program, with possible promotions in support; or will our money go primarily into a promotion such as a sponsorship (for example, racing sponsorship for a motor oil), with advertising in support. More often the primary communication will be message oriented, usually advertising or direct mail, but not always.

Once we have answered this question, a general Primary Creative Brief is prepared, along with secondary Creative Briefs as necessary. Representatives from each of the important vendors who will be involved in the programs should be involved in the preparation of the primary creative brief. The vendor for the primary communication option has the ultimate responsibility, of course, along with the marketer, but involving everyone ensures that from the very beginning everyone understands where the campaign is headed. As anyone who has been involved in putting together a creative brief knows, the process can be long and involved. Everyone has an opinion. However, if everyone has read the IMC plan and studies the IMC Task Grid, the discussion should be much more focused.

By having everyone involved from the start, once the primary creative brief has been completed, each of the vendors will have a clear idea of the job to be done, and creative thinking will be directed toward a common objective.

Implementing Consistent Creative

As we have suggested, and as you might imagine, this is not a simple task. But it can be done, and when it is, a truly effective IMC program results. To help better understand how to accomplish all of this, let us consider an example. Suppose a bank wishes to increase the use of telephone banking among their customer base. Since the primary target audience is the bank's customers, you might think the best way to reach them is with a promotion. While it is true that advertising would not be the primary medium, the primary communications should still be message oriented. In this case the message would be delivered via direct mail.

This is an important distinction to note. You may think of direct mail as "promotion" because it is not advertising in the traditional sense. But in this case, because we wish to build a strong positive brand attitude for telephone banking, we are "advertising." We are simply using direct mail to target the bank's customers. This is a good example of how the old understanding of advertising and promotion must change in IMC planning.

Since we want a message-oriented program, we need a general creative brief for the various message-oriented executions that will be needed. Figure 4.4 presents a hypothetical primary creative brief for message-oriented executions in this example. We shall assume that it has been developed hand-in-hand with the responsible people from the involved vendors. We might imagine in this case that it is the direct mail agency, along with those responsible for collateral and merchandising, as well as the advertising agency.

Why include the advertising agency if there is to be no advertising as such? Representatives of the advertising agency should always be present when *any* creative brief is being considered, because *every* campaign must be consistent with the overall marketing communication program. While this creative brief is for telephone banking among the bank's checking account customers, it must "fit" the bank's overall marketing communications look and feel, and most certainly be consistent and compatible with the bank's general checking account advertising.

Looking at the primary creative brief shown in Figure 4.4, we see this point highlighted. The primary communications objective (in terms of brand attitude) is to "reinforce convenience positioning." This means the overall positioning for the bank's retail services is *convenience*, and telephone banking must be shown as compatible with this overall

Figure 4.4		
Primary Communication Creative Brief for Message-Oriented IMC		
PRODUCT Telephone Banking	**JOB**	**DATE**
KEY MARKET OBSERVATIONS Potential customers are probably going into branches to conduct business that could be done over the phone		
SOURCE OF BUSINESS Current bank checking account customers		
CONSUMER INSIGHT They are willing to use electronic devices, and are heavy users of ATMs		
TARGET MARKET Young and middle income "full nest" households with busy lives		
COMMUNICATION OBJECTIVES AND TASKS Brand attitude primary objective seeking to reinforce overall IMC convenience positioning		
BRAND ATTITUDE STRATEGY Low involvement/informational brand attitude strategy driven by motivation of incomplete satisfaction		
BENEFIT CLAIM AND SUPPORT Telephone banking is more convenient. Support: pay bills almost any time as well as transact basic banking business at any time.		
DESIRED CONSUMER RESPONSE See that telephone banking really is more convenient than branch banking and try it		
CREATIVE GUIDELINES Tie "inconvenience" of banking to awareness of telephone banking (recall); consider exaggeration in execution		
REQUIREMENTS/MANDATORY CONTENT Required legal identifications		

positioning. Those writing the direct mail copy must understand this, and should be supplied with the current bank marketing communications in support of that positioning. The direct mail will be different, making its own key benefit claim with appropriate support, but it will be consistent with the look and "feel" of the overall marketing communication program.

This same general creative brief will be used by the creative people developing the collateral and merchandising material to be used in the bank branches. But here is where we encounter another problem in effectively implementing a consistent IMC program. How can we be sure their executions, based upon this creative brief, will be consistent with the look and "feel" of the direct mail? Here is where IMC central planning at the bank is crucial. Initial plans for what collateral and merchandising materials will be needed, and the initial drafting of copy, can proceed after the general creative brief is ready. But final executions must await the development of the direct mail.

It will be up to those charged with managing the IMC campaign at the *marketer* (the bank in our example) to see to it that each vendor works within the look and "feel" of the overall marketing communication program and the general creative brief, and that the secondary components of each campaign are consistent with the primary creative executions. This process is outlined in the flow chart shown in Figure 4.5.

Within the campaign there may also be one or more secondary communication tasks that are more tactical in nature. These will require their own secondary creative brief. Continuing our telephone banking example, it may be decided that in addition to the message-oriented marketing communication, a promotion to stimulate immediate response is also desired. A hypothetical secondary creative brief for a sweepstakes promotion is illustrated in Figure 4.6. Obviously the

Figure 4.5
Managing IMC Creative Executions

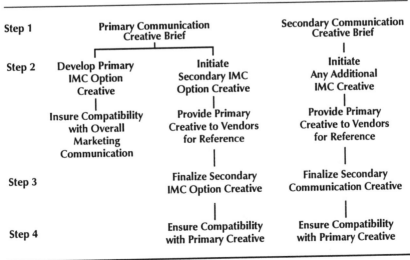

Step 1	**Primary Communication Creative Brief**	**Secondary Communication Creative Brief**
Step 2	**Develop Primary IMC Option Creative** / **Initiate Secondary IMC Option Creative**	**Initiate Any Additional IMC Creative**
	Insure Compatibility with Overall Marketing Communication / **Provide Primary Creative to Vendors for Reference**	**Provide Primary Creative to Vendors for Reference**
Step 3	**Finalize Secondary IMC Option Creative**	**Finalize Secondary Communication Creative**
Step 4	**Ensure Compatibility with Primary Creative**	**Ensure Compatibility with Primary Creative**

Figure 4.6

Secondary Communication Creative Brief for Promotion-Oriented IMC

PRODUCT Telephone Banking	JOB Sweepstakes	DATE
KEY MARKET OBSERVATIONS Potential customers are probably going into branches to conduct business that could be done over the phone		
SOURCE OF BUSINESS Current bank checking account customers		
CONSUMER INSIGHT They are willing to use electronic devices, and are heavy users of ATMs		
TARGET MARKET Young and middle income "full nest" households with busy lives		
COMMUNICATION OBJECTIVES AND TASKS Brand purchase intention is primary objective, seeking immediate sign-up for telephone banking		
BRAND ATTITUDE STRATEGY Low involvement/informational brand attitude strategy driven by motivation of incomplete satisfaction		
BENEFIT CLAIM AND SUPPORT Limited time customer sweepstakes. Support: chance to win when you sign up for telephone banking, and extra chances to win each time used		
DESIRED CONSUMER RESPONSE Enter sweepstakes immediately by signing up for telephone banking, then see how telephone banking really is more convenient		
CREATIVE GUIDELINES Remain consistent with primary communication creative and overall IMC convenient positiioning		
REQUIREMENTS/MANDATORY CONTENT Usual sweepstakes and banking legal notice		

background section of the creative brief is identical. But since this is a short-term tactical promotion, the primary communication objective (this time in terms of brand purchase intention) is "immediate sign-up for telephone banking." This creative brief will be given to the promotion vendor designing the sweepstakes. Just as with the secondary communication tasks associated with the message-oriented part of the campaign, the final executions for the sweepstakes must await the creation of the direct mail executions.

Consistent creative products are an essential feature of successful IMC. To achieve this consistency requires careful attention and management on the part of the marketer. This is what IMC planning is all about, the effective coordination of various marketing communication tasks to optimize your marketing communication strategy. At the heart of IMC planning is a manager who assumes this responsibility. It is up to this manager to supervise the work of the various marketing communication vendors, seeing to it that all work is consistent with the creative brief, and that the executions for the secondary communication tasks are consistent with the look and "feel" of the primary communication executions.

Chapter Notes

[1] R. A. Strang, *The Promotional Planning Process* (New York: Praeger, 1980).

[2] D. E. Schultz, "Traditional Advertising Has Role to Play in IMC," *Marketing News*, August 28, 1995: 18.

[3] W. T. Moran, "Insights from Pricing Research," in E. B. Bailey (Ed.), *Pricing Practices and Strategies* (New York: The Conference Board, 1978), 7–13.

CHAPTER FIVE

Selecting Promotion Tactics

When most people think about promotion they are usually thinking about what has traditionally been called "sales promotion." This is generally defined as any direct purchasing incentive, reward, or promise that is given to your target audience for making a specific purchase or taking a specific action that will benefit those responding to the promotion. Later we will be taking a close look at several basic consumer and trade promotion techniques that certainly fit this traditional definition, but for IMC planning we really must look beyond this traditional understanding of sales promotion.

To begin with, our understanding of promotion includes a wide variety of techniques that help accelerate normal purchase behavior. We should have a good feel for just what a promotion can and should be from the last chapter. Rossiter and Percy[1] have introduced an interesting and important consideration in how one should think about promotions: the notion of *time*. Consistent with the importance of understanding how consumers make purchase or usage decisions (as exemplified by the Behavioral Sequence Model, for example), they remind us that promotion techniques should be integrated over time in relation to the target audience's decision process. Recalling our generic BSM, this suggests that some promotional techniques may be helpful prior to the actual purchase or use of a product or service during need arousal or information search and evaluation, some during the purchase, others after purchase.

This, of course, was implied by the IMC Task Grid. You will remember that communication options are considered for each step in the decision process. Specific promotional techniques should be considered for each step, but it is not necessary to always include a promotion. Promotion may be inappropriate at any one step, or while appropriate, may not be the best place to spend your marketing dollars. If a promotion makes sense in order to accelerate the decision process, we must choose one that fits.

When we think of promotion in this general way, not just as sales promotion, but as part of our marketing communication when we want to speed up the decision process, it is impossible to consider a promotion in isolation. How can a promotion help achieve our communication objectives? As we review our IMC Task Grid in developing an IMC program, we should be thinking about whether a particular type of promotion will be an effective part of the *whole* marketing communication effort.

As we have been underscoring all along, this is what we mean by IMC—looking at all available communication options and using those that best help us effectively and efficiently meet our objectives.

Basic Types of Promotion

Promotions are generally divided into two broad categories: immediate reward promotions and delayed reward promotions. Immediate reward promotions are offers that provide something now, such as price reductions, bonus packs, free gifts with a purchase, and so on. Delayed reward promotions defer the benefit of the promotion, and usually require the target audience to do something before they receive the benefit of the promotion. These would include such things as sweepstakes, refund offers that require a proof-of-purchase, frequent flyer programs, and so on. Generally speaking, immediate reward promotions are usually more effective because of their immediacy. This, of course, is consistent with the primary use of promotions to influence action *now*.

When we think of promotions we usually are thinking of consumer promotions, but promotions can be directed at the sales force and trade as well. In reality there are at least three major types of promotion that we must consider: trade, retail, and consumer.

Trade Promotion

Overall, about half of all marketing communications dollars are spent as trade promotion. Trade spending increased significantly through the 1980s, from about one-third of all marketing communication dollars in 1981 to half in 1991, although there is some indication that this upward trend is about to reverse itself.[2] Generally speaking, a trade promotion is a program of discounts aimed at increasing distribution or some sort of merchandising activity at the retail level. This may include everything from slotting allowances to sales incentives designed to reward individual retail salespeople for meeting specific sales goals. Later we shall look specifically at three basic trade promotion techniques.

Retail Promotion

To the customer, there is not much of a difference between a retail promotion and a consumer promotion (described below). All they see is a price incentive or special display. In both cases an inducement is offered to accelerate the decision process. But from a planning standpoint, there is a crucial difference. Retail promotions are generally independent of the manufacturer, initiated either by the distributor or the retailer. This often puts retail promotion outside the scope of IMC planning. To help bring retail promotion within at least the planning control of the manufacturer, more companies are turning to something called *tactical marketing*, which we shall discuss in Chapter 6.

Consumer Promotion

Consumer promotions are developed by the manufacturer or its agency and directed toward the target audience in order to accelerate the decision process. Often these promotions are experienced at the retail level. Shelf-talkers (those messages you find actually attached to a shelf in the store), in-store coupons or bonus-packs, special displays, price-off offers—all are received at the point of purchase. But what makes them different from what could be an identical-looking retail promotion is that it was initiated by the manufacturer, not the retailer.

The importance of coordinating retail and consumer promotion is underscored by the finding of a recent study of consumer perceptions of promotional activity. In this study it was found that "many consumers are reasonably accurate about deal frequency and sale price."[3] This is significant in light of the general notion in consumer behavior literature that consumers tend to plan their brand choices and how much they buy based upon when they expect a promotion. If consumers "sense" when a product or service is likely to be on promotion, they are not making a distinction between a retail and consumer promotion. But, the retail promotion will certainly be a factor in the consumer's purchase or usage plans. If the manufacturer does not control or at least track these promotions, there is the potential for conflict between the promotion objectives of the retail store and the manufacturer. So even if a retailer insists upon control of their promotions, it is essential that you stay informed about them and do your best to influence the message content and execution.

Six Basic Consumer Promotion Techniques

As we can see in Figure 5.1, there are six basic types of consumer promotion techniques. These include refunds and rebates, sampling, loyalty or loading devices, couponing, premiums, and sweepstakes, games, and contests. We will look at each of these types of promotion techniques below. There are, of course many others, everything from the product itself to unique applications of the distribution channel. But for our purposes we will only be considering these six basic techniques.

Figure 5.1
Six Basic Sales Promotion Techniques

BASIC TECHNIQUE	EXAMPLES
1. Refunds and Rebates	Automobile rebates used to lower initial purchase price, mail-in proof of purchase for refund
2. Sampling	Direct mailing of trial size, door-to-door or street intercept distribution of product, mail-in coupon for free product
3. Loyalty and Loading Devices	Multiple or bonus packs, price-off packs, continuity programs, viz., frequent flyer
4. Couponing	Coupons delivered for reduced price via FSI, magazines, direct mail, on or in package
5. Premiums	Product-associated premiums like Marlboro Western wear, product as premiums, reusable container
6. Sweepstakes, Games, and Contests	Free product or trips for mail-in participation, entry for accepting product demonstration, "scratch" cards to save for prizes

Refunds and Rebates

A refund or rebate promotion is an offer that is made by a marketer to refund a certain amount of money, send a coupon, or provide an additional product or some other premium as a result of purchasing a product, on the basis of proof-of-purchase. While most refunds and rebates are made directly to the consumer, they can be passed along by the retailer (for example automobile rebates used to lower the initial purchase price). These refunds and rebates can be either a specific dollar amount or a portion of the actual retail value of the product, ranging from a certain percentage all the way up to a full refund of the purchasing price. Refunds and rebates are used to encourage purchase or trial of a product, to reward loyal users, to prevent switching, and so on. There are a number of ways of delivering this promotion message, everything from direct mail, FSIs (free standing inserts in newspapers or magazines), in or on the package, and even advertising. The most common use for refunds or rebates is as a temporary sales stimulus or as a defensive measure to help counteract some competitive activity. Some of the strengths of using refunds or rebates include such things as:

- It effectively reduces the price *without* using the retailer

- It can be especially useful in stimulating interest in high-priced products or services

- There is a high level of non-redemption among those intending to, reducing overall cost

On the other hand, the value of refunds or rebates to the consumer is delayed, and somewhat limited in appeal. Many people perceive the effort involved as "not worth it."

Sampling

Sampling is when the target audience is given an opportunity to actually try or use the product with little or no cost. It can range from an actual product sample either in a regular size or a special sample size that has been developed for the promotion, to the use of a product or service for a limited time (for example, a 30-day trial offer). The objective of sampling is to encourage trial and repeat purchase of a product or service with a broader consumer base for an established product or service. Because of market and media fragmentation, and the high cost of buying shelf space in stores, sampling is expected to grow in popularity. Donnelly estimates that sampling is now used by 64 percent of manufacturers.[4] Products with low trial or a demonstrable product difference are ideal candidates for sampling.

Samples can be delivered in a variety of ways, each with its own particular advantages and disadvantages. For example, sampling in-store or at a central location has the advantage of low distribution cost, but it is difficult to control who receives the sample. Direct mail offers an effective way of sampling either a broadly based target market or a highly targeted market (see Chapter 6), but there are obvious limits to what you can efficiently sample through the mail. Door-to-door offers the only means of sampling products containing hazardous ingredients, but it tends to be inefficient and expensive.

Overall, the most effective way of reaching a broadly based target market is with direct mail. In-store sampling is less expensive, but offers a more limited reach. Using advertising media to "invite" people to call or write for a sample is ideal for low budgets, but again has a very limited reach.

Loyalty and Loading Devices

Loyalty devices are promotions that are designed to reward the target audience for being loyal to a brand. They are designed to build repeat purchase for the brand and have the advantage of enabling you to develop a strong database on your loyal customers, which in turn can be used to monitor satisfaction over a period of time. We will be discussing databases in the next chapter. Loading promotions differ in that they are designed to take consumers out of their normal purchasing pattern by encouraging the purchase of such things as a larger size, a special bonus offer, or multiple packs. The reasons for wanting to do this can range from trying to upgrade the value or revenue of a purchase to a defensive measure against competitive strategy.

Some of the more common ways of implementing loyalty or loading promotions are such things as bonus packs, cents-off and price-packs, and continuity programs. *Bonus packs* are a particularly effective technique for moving additional product to the consumer. *Cents-off* and *price-packs* are an extremely effective and efficient promotion technique, especially where the opportunity exists to stimulate brand switching, and as a strong defensive move when one is needed quickly.

Continuity programs are promotions that require the consumer to do something like save stamps, coupons, or proofs-of-purchase over a period of time in order to accumulate enough to qualify for a gift, trip, or a reward of some kind. Perhaps the best known promotions of this kind are the frequent flyer programs of major airlines. But, increasingly, major packaged goods companies such as Kraft General Foods, Proctor & Gamble, Johnson & Johnson, and others are building and using a database to increase loyalty to their brands.[5] The objective of continuity programs is to hold onto current users and to encourage occasional users to become more frequent users.

Again, however, we must consider the strengths and weakness of the various loyalty-building and loading devices available to us. Bonus packs, for example, while creating an immediate incentive to buy because the "bonus" is immediate, are unpopular with the trade because they interfere with normal stocking and take up extra shelf space without adding additional profit for the store. Cents-off and special price-packs (where the discounted price is specifically marked on the package by the manufacturer) again offer an immediate value at the point of purchase, but tend to subsidize regular users more than encourage new trial or switching. Continuity programs do a good job of retaining customers and help build brand loyalty, but they do require long-term commitment on the part of both the target market and the manufacturer, who may find the cost in the long run much greater than expected.

Couponing

There are two types of coupons, manufacturer sponsored (consumer promotion), and distributor and store sponsored and distributed (retail promotion). As we mentioned earlier, however, this is not a distinction a consumer is likely to make, but one that must be considered in IMC planning. Basically, couponing is an effective promotion technique that utilizes a variety of means for distributing cents off. Coupons are an excellent way of inducing trial for a new product and also to encourage repeat purchase. There is a danger in using coupons, however. Over 80 percent of coupon users stockpile coupons for the same brand, effectively lowering the price for all of their purchases of the brand.

A growing trend in the use of coupons is more targeted couponing. Donnelly finds that 75 percent of those using promotions use direct mail couponing, 62 percent use ethnic promotions, and 55 percent use electronic couponing. They predict that marketers will increasingly vary copy or cents-off values geodemographically, or even at the household level.[6]

While there are some indications that marketers may be taking a harder look at the cost of using coupons, and that overall coupon distribution levels may have peaked, or even begun to drop slightly,[7] they remain very popular with shoppers. In fact, consumers hold more favorable attitudes toward grocery product brands that offer coupons or other price incentives, and that feeling has been increasing. Nearly all households in a 1992 study reported both using coupons at least sometimes, and feeling they are either very or somewhat helpful.[8] In another study conducted in 1993, 72 percent of primary shoppers reported using coupons as a way to save money on grocery bills, and 55 percent said they use them to help plan their shopping.[9]

Even though only 2 or 3 percent of the more than 300 billion coupons that are distributed each year are ever redeemed, coupons remain an important promotion option. One of the suggested reasons for a possible decline in coupon redemption is a significant shortening of expiration periods in an effort by marketers to control coupon liability. According to the coupon clearing house CMS Inc., in 1993 the average redemption period was 3.8 months, about one-half the time allowed six years earlier.[10]

Traditionally, coupons have been distributed via direct mail and newspaper FSIs or other print advertising. Occasionally, too, coupons are included in packages of the couponed or sister brands. But as technology increases in both stores and homes, the use of electronic couponing will become more prevalent. An on-line electronic coupon program service is now available for home computers. All the consumers must do is select the coupons they want and print them out.

Looking at the relative advantages of the primary delivery media for coupons, FSIs offer quick delivery at about half the cost of direct mail, but relatively no selectivity in reach. Coupons printed in advertising offer some selectivity in target audience, but a generally lower redemption rate. Direct mail offers highly selective and targeted distribution, but relative to other media is more expensive.

Premiums

There are numerous types of premiums and just as many ways of delivering them. The goal of premiums is to influence consumers to take a specific action or actions, with the premium as a reward. For the consumer, premiums are typically used when a strong trial-inducing device is needed.

There are a wide variety of premiums one might consider. But it is very important to remember that the premium must appeal to the target audience, and they must perceive a value in the offer. Premiums may be offered in connection with a one-time purchase or as part of a continuity program. The premium may require a mailed response, or be available at the point of purchase.

Mail-in premiums have the advantage of rewarding current users, but they must wait for the reward, and to be effective this type of promotion requires advertising. When a premium is part of a package, it has the advantages of attracting attention to the product (usually with the enticement "FREE!") and the reward is immediate, but it can occasion packaging problems and additional distribution costs. When a promotion is available at the time of purchase (but not in or on the package), it too offers an immediate reward to the consumer and permits one to offer larger premiums, but it does require significant retailer support.

Premiums may also be "self-liquidating." This is where a premium is made available at a reduced price, usually 30 to 50 percent below regular retail prices, enough to cover the out-of-pocket cost of the merchandise. While a self-liquidating premium is generally a low-cost promotion, and able to selectively target consumers via the type of premium offered, it does require advertising support to generate interest, and the reward is not immediate.

Sweepstakes, Games, and Contests

Sweepstakes, games, and contests offer the consumer a chance to win a cash prize, merchandise, or travel in return for using the promoted brand or taking a specific action, such as visiting a dealer for a demonstration. Generally they are used to create awareness for the brand or to provide a unifying theme for a group of promotions.

A significant concern with sweepstakes, games, and contests that is less of a problem with other types of consumer promotion is the legal aspects. As an attorney specializing in this area has put it, once you have decided upon your objectives and what type of sweepstakes, game, or contest might satisfy those objectives, the next step is to involve a legal expert. While we do not want to get into details (something outside the scope of this book), perhaps it would be useful to relate some of the advice this attorney offers marketers in order to provide a sense of the potential complications involved.

The most important thing from a legal standpoint is the official rules of the promotion. So if you run an annual promotion, even if you feel it is basically the same as last year's, it is better to check. Even seemingly insignificant changes may mean a new law applies. It is impossible to include a full set of rules on a package or in advertising, but an abbreviated set of the official rules must appear. In fact, "rules for a TV ad that mentions a consumer sweepstakes should, at a minimum, include the following information: (1) no purchase necessary; (2) void where prohibited; (3) any age and geographic limitations for eligibility; (4) an end date for the sweepstakes; (5) that the sweepstakes is subject to complete official rules; (6) how consumers may obtain a copy of those rules; and (7) the name and address of the sponsor."[11] Clearly, this is an area where expert help is required.

There are real weaknesses to sweepstakes, games, and contests as a part of an IMC program, but where they do work, they can help reinforce the image of a product or service at a relatively low cost. When well conceived they can also create excitement and interest. But they do not require a purchase, and the reward is not only usually delayed, but also limited to only a small number of participants.

Brand Equity Implications for Consumer Promotion

In Chapter 2 we discussed the relative advantages of advertising and promotion in satisfying our basic communication objectives. You will remember that brand attitude was the primary strength of advertising, but that we mentioned well-conceived promotion executions not only could, but should address brand attitude objectives. There is no reason why one cannot use promotion to enhance brand equity via communicating a positive brand attitude consistent with a product or service's brand positioning. To quote Chuck Mittelstadt, long-time consultant to the Interpublic Group of Companies, "Promotions must be as creative as image advertising, and fully as effective in building brand equity."[12]

Each of the six basic consumer promotion techniques just reviewed offer opportunities for enhancing brand equity.

Refunds and Rebates

Offers made through traditional advertising media have a built-in opportunity of integrating the promotion and advertising message. Also, any offer that requires clipping a "certificate" provides a means of delivering the key benefit claims on the refund certificate itself. The offer itself should be worded in a positive way, linked to the product or service, and *unique*. Too often very little imagination is used in a refund or rebate offer. Most automotive rebate offers, for example, usually offer nothing more than something like: "Get $1,000 back!" You want to avoid the impression that this is just another price-off deal. Try to relate the offer to something positive, such as your confidence in the product or service.

Sampling

In sampling we have a promotion technique that in itself should stimulate a positive brand attitude. The consumer is being offered something for nothing, and especially for new products, this provides an opportunity to quickly establish brand attitude. In one sense a person is already at least somewhat favorably inclined toward the product or service or they would not accept and use the sample. The packaging and representation of the sample itself also offers an opportunity for building brand equity.

Loyalty and Loading Devices

Like sampling, most loyalty and loading devices automatically affect brand attitude positioning—or should! Loading devices such as bonus packs and cents-off or price-packs do *not* automatically contribute to an increase in positive brand attitude, and when misused (for example when offered too frequently) can have a *negative* effect upon brand equity. How? If a brand has a premium image yet is often seen in price-packs, it will assume a lower-price image; even a regular-priced brand can suffer from too frequent use of cents-off price-packs. This is, of course, true of *any* price promotion if it is used too often, but especially with loading devices because the lower price is visually reinforced on the package.

Bonus packs offer a better opportunity, especially when the "bonus" is offered by way of a larger package. This offers an opportunity on the package label to reinforce brand attitude, which coupled with the positive reward of the "bonus," should nurture or increase brand equity. If multiple unit packaging is used, while the wrapper does offer some opportunity for reinforcing brand attitude message, it will be discarded with use. Consideration should be given to a special package as well so the initial favorable attitude stimulated by the multiple bonus pack at the point of purchase will be reinforced each time the consumer uses the product.

Loyalty or continuity programs build positive brand attitude, and hence brand equity, in a different fashion. By their very nature, such programs require product use over time before rewards are forthcoming. This provides a good opportunity for "reminding" the consumer of the coming reward within a positive brand attitude message, either on the package, through advertising, or through direct mail. On the other hand, if the requirements for earning a reward are seen as too difficult, or if the rules change over time, this can have serious negative consequences for brand equity. In the mid-1990s airline frequent flyer programs found themselves in just such a bind. Not only did reward levels become more difficult to reach, but it became more and more difficult to actually use frequent flyer "points" for free flights because of high demand for seats. As a result, participants felt "trapped" in a program and "cheated" by the airlines, seriously affecting the brand equity of the airlines among their most loyal customers.

Coupons

Coupons are frequently used to introduce a new or "improved" product, and as such help initiate a positive brand attitude. But to be effective, coupons should be tied to the introductory advertising. This helps channel the good "feeling" occasioned by being offered a chance to try the new product at a discount with a positive message about the product itself. Even when used as a short-term tactic with established brands, this good feeling will occur as long as the coupon is not expected. When a brand regularly uses coupons they are no longer seen as a "gift" from the company, but merely as the means of sustaining a lower price.

Regardless of whether a coupon is used for a new or established product, it is important to carry over the key benefit claim from the advertising to the coupon itself. If you are not currently advertising the brand, the key benefit from the product or service's positioning should be conveyed on the coupons. This connects the positive reward of the discount with the brand's key benefit claim, reinforcing positive brand attitude. Additionally, this message is reinforced each time the coupon is "reviewed" by the consumer, right up until it is surrendered at the store.

Premiums

Ideally a premium is chosen to reinforce the choice of the original product or service, appealing to the same motivation as the product or service. For positively motivated behavior this means reinforcing the user's image. Almost anything that will be seen by others and carries the brand's logo will help reinforce user brand attitude because it announces to the world the user's brand choice. Everything from jackets or other apparel with the brand's logo to things like insulated holders for beer cans might be used, but it is important that the premium be consistent with the image projected by the brand.

Negatively motivated behavior calls for premiums that are more directly related to the product or service offering the premium. For example, special folders for storing insurance policies or sun visors with a sunscreen provide positive, long-running association with the brand. As with positively motivated products, these premiums also should include the company logo or brand name. In this case it is to remind the user of the brand, not necessarily to be noticed by others.

Selecting premiums congruent with motivations ensures positive brand attitude and the nurturing of brand equity. The most common mistake marketers make in selecting premiums is not relating them to the brand itself in a meaningful way and making certain they appeal to the same motivation that drives choice of the brand. But the biggest mistake a marketer can make is to offer a premium that is either inappropriate or unappealing to the target market. This may lead to negative attitudes toward the brand and a weakening of the brand's equity.

Sweepstakes, Games, and Contests

One of the more subtle benefits of a sweepstakes or contest promotion is that by its very nature it attracts people to the advertising or other source of announcing the promotion. This is itself a good opportunity for associating the promotion with a strong brand attitude message. Beyond this, the sweepstakes, games, or contests themselves should be created around the brand's perceived benefits. The stronger the link between the motivations associated with the product or service and the promotion, the more likely it will be reinforcing a positive brand attitude and corresponding brand equity.

When to Use Specific Consumer Promotions

Back in Chapter 2 we talked generally about communication objectives for both advertising and promotion, and in Chapter 4 we looked more specifically at the strengths of promotion versus advertising. In this section we will review briefly some of the situations in which particular consumer promotions might be an effective part of an IMC program.

One of the first strategic considerations we discussed was whether our overall objective was trial or repeat purchase. As we see in Figure 5.2, three of the basic consumer promotions are generally best suited for generating trial, three for repeat purchase. The trial promotions are refunds and rebates, sampling, and coupons. The repeat purchase promotions are loyalty and loading devices, premiums, and sweepstakes, games, and contests.

Before we review some of the situations where different promotions might be effective, it would be well to point out that since promotions are generally used in a tactical sense to accelerate brand purchase intention, there are many, many unique ways such promotions might be applied. All we are attempting to do here is outline some of the conditions where a particular type of consumer promotion might be applicable. This should help further distinguish the particular strengths of the various types of basic consumer promotions.

Trial Promotion Applications

While refunds and rebates, sampling, and coupons are especially effective in generating trial, this is not to say they are ineffective as usage promotions. Strategically, however, when trial is our objective, these three promotions should be considered. Of the three, sampling is probably the most effective promotion for generating trial, followed closely by coupons. Refunds and rebates, because they are less immediate, are somewhat less effective. But, they are perhaps the best means of accelerating trial of expensive products or services. They are also very useful in defending against strong competitors when the purchase cycle for the category is long.

Sampling is particularly effective where category or brand trial is low, especially if your brand has a demonstrable difference that will be readily

---

Figure 5.2
Best Consumer Promotions to Generate Trial and Repeat Purchase

Trial Promotions	Refunds and Rebates
	Sampling
	Coupons
Repeat Purchase Promotions	Loyalty and Loading Devices
	Premiums
	Sweepstakes, Games, and Contests

apparent with use. It is also a good way of beating the competition to the punch when a new category is being introduced. As potential users consider a new category, sampling helps "push" them into action, and with your brand. Sampling is also an effective technique when advertising may not be able to effectively demonstrate your brand's advantage. Is your hand lotion really less messy? Is your crust really crispier? Do you really feel relief faster? If using your product or service easily and quickly shows a positive benefit, sampling can be an effective way of making benefit claims believable.

While couponing is less effective than sampling in generating trial, it has the advantage of being much less expensive. The introduction of a new product or service is an ideal time to use coupons in stimulating trial, or when you want to attract new users to the brand. The problem here, of course, is that current users will use the coupon as well. Figure 5.3 reviews favorable situations for trial promotions.

Repeat Purchase Promotion Applications

Strategic application of repeat purchase promotion tends to address more short-term issues than trial promotions do. Trial promotions are meant to bring in new customers for the long-term health of the brand. Repeat purchase promotions are generally used to alter the timing of purchase, capturing users in the short term to take them out of the market. How-

Figure 5.3
Favorable Situations for Trial Promotions

BASIC TECHNIQUE	FAVORABLE SITUATIONS
Refunds and Rebates	Good for expensive products or services
	To defend against strong competitor
Sampling	Use for products with low trial and a demonstrable difference
	Good for new product category introduction
	When advertising cannot adequately demonstrate brand benefit
Coupons	Good for low budgets
	Good for new product introduction

ever, when well executed, usage promotions should also help enhance positive brand attitude and lead to a stronger brand equity in the long run.

Of the repeat purchase promotions we discussed, loyalty or continuity programs are the ones most directly aimed at creating and maintaining brand loyalty. The others are aimed at people who tend to switch among various brands, with the intention of attracting them to our brand on their next category purchase. Again, if we execute the promotion with brand equity in mind, we will be building a more positive attitude toward our brand, the result being more frequent switching to our brand.

All repeat purchase promotions, but especially premiums, can be conceived in a manner to target particular segments of a market. The appeal of the premium can easily be matched to particular audiences, as can the prizes in sweepstakes, games, and contests. Both premiums and sweepstakes, games, and contests also have the potential of generating in-store merchandising activity such as point-of-purchase display, banners, special displays, and so on. This has the advantage of both drawing switchers' attention to the brand as well as the opportunity of reinforcing benefit claims. Sweepstakes, games, and contests also present a good way of providing a unifying theme for an IMC campaign.

Loyalty programs, and especially loading devices, are a good way of defending against competitor activity by removing people from the market. Loyalty programs help hold current brand loyal customers and retain switchers by building repeat purchase or use. Loading devices such as price-packs and bonus packs help attract switchers to our brand, and retard switching out to other brands. However, this can only be seen as a short-term, tactical application. For example, if you know a competitor is about to launch a new brand or otherwise challenge your product, a bonus pack will temporarily disrupt this introduction by reducing category demand.

Repeat purchase promotions can be very effective, but one must guard against using them in a predictable or ongoing way (with the exception of loyalty programs, of course). They are meant to stimulate short-term usage, but they can also produce a more positive brand attitude. As with all promotions, we want them to contribute to long-term growth. Figure 5.4 reviews favorable situations for repeat purchase promotions.

Three Basic Trade Promotion Techniques

We have already noted that spending in trade promotion accounts for about half of all marketing communications money spent, about twice that spent on consumer promotions. This trend is a function of many

Figure 5.4
Favorable Situations for Repeat Purchase Promotions

BASIC TECHNIQUE	FAVORABLE SITUATIONS
Loyalty and Loading Devices	To defend against switching
	When a new competitor is about to enter the category
Premiums	Good for selective appeal
	Encourage point-of-purchase display
Sweepstakes, Games, and Contests	Provide unifying theme for group of promotions
	Gain in-store merchandising activity
	Reinforce positioning and advertising message

things, including a growing understanding on the part of the trade of their power in the mix. But perhaps the key reason has been the short-run emphasis of too many marketers using promotion to "buy share" in order to satisfy immediate sales goals.

We cannot emphasize enough that this is *not* the way to deal with trade promotion. It is certainly true that without good distribution consumers do not have an opportunity to purchase. But you must remember that your goals and the goals of the trade are not always the same. The trade makes its money from *category* sales. They are indifferent to what brands sell as long as their margins for the category are sustained. You, of course, are interested only in the sales of your brand.

So, while trade promotion must be seen as a cost of doing business, strategically it must be considered within your overall IMC planning. This means integrating trade promotion with consumer promotion and advertising. Figure 5.5 details a number of trade promotions. As we already mentioned, trade promotions are usually a short-term incentive or deal that's offered to retailers or some other key participant in the distribution channel to stimulate stocking an item or to feature and/or promote a product or service. These promotions depend entirely on trade cooperation for any product sales increase.

Figure 5.5
Three Basic Trade Promotion Techniques

BASIC TECHNIQUE	EXAMPLES
Allowance Promotions	• Slotting allowances
	• Performance allowances
	• Trade coupons
	• Free product
Display Material Promotions	• Point-of-purchase
	• Special display
Trade Premiums and Incentives	• Dealer loaders
	• Incentive programs

Success with any product depends upon trade or dealer support. The purpose of trade promotions is to in some fashion improve relations with the trade to gain and hold new distribution, build trade inventories, or obtain trade merchandising support. There are three principal classifications of trade-oriented sales promotions:

- Allowance promotions

- Display material promotions

- Trade premiums and incentives

Allowance promotions offer the trade something in return for purchasing or promoting a specific quantity of a product or service, or for meeting specific buying or performance requirements. *Display material promotions* provide the trade or dealer with special in-store display material to use in featuring the promoted product or service, often in conjunction with a trade allowance promotion. *Trade premiums and incentives* are promotions that offer the trade a free gift or a chance for an even higher value prize in return for purchasing specific quantities of goods or meeting certain specified requirements.

Before we discuss these three basic types of trade promotion in more detail, it will be good to point out that there are both trial and repeat purchase trade promotions, just as with consumer promotions. Trial trade promotions are largely designed to gain an acceptance of a new product, or get the trade to begin carrying an existing one. Slotting fees are an example of a trial trade promotion. While one can understand that with an ever-increasing demand to handle new products and line extensions, and their high failure rate, the trade is demanding some help to deal with the flow and overhead, the high fees charged are worrisome. It has been estimated that as much as 70 percent of slotting allowances go directly to the retailer bottom line rather than to defraying costs.

Repeat purchase trade promotions are used to ensure a product is stocked, as well as to get favorable shelf space. Various allowances are obvious repeat purchase promotions. Actually, all three types of trade promotion have application as repeat purchase promotion.

Allowances

Allowances to the trade can take many forms, everything from direct price reductions on invoices to free goods. We have already mentioned slotting allowances, and their virtual necessity for achieving distribution of a consumer packaged good product. As such fees increase, it makes it more and more difficult for those with small marketing budgets to compete.

A general weakness of most trade promotional allowances is that there is no guarantee that any significant portion of the money will find its way to the consumer, either through increased merchandising activity or lower prices. This is true of buying allowances, performance allowances, and even free goods. As a result, while it is very important that trade and consumer support be integrated, one must consider any consumer benefit a plus. Rather, trade allowances should be used for tactical purposes with the trade. For example, buying allowances and free goods help build inventories in support of consumer marketing programs (both promotion and advertising). Performance allowances, at least in part, will go to merchandising or retail advertising in support of the brand.

Trade coupons are actually coupons for the consumer, but distributed by the retailer rather than the manufacturer. They differ from retail promotions in that trade coupons are controlled by the marketer, not the retailer. Usually, the retailer pays for distributing the coupon in their advertising or flyers and then is reimbursed by the marketer after the promotion. Because consumer promotions with coupons are keyed to trial, the same is true for trade coupons. Only in this case it is not trial by the trade, but by the consumer. Actually, it is a repeat purchase promotion for the trade, in the same sense as the other allowances we have discussed.

This is an important point for IMC planning. Retailers as a rule like trade coupons because they help extend their own marketing communication budget. In this sense trade coupons can help secure trade cooperation within an IMC program. That is step one. But step two is the consumer response to the coupons. This must be considered in light of everything discussed about coupons as a consumer trial promotion.

Display Materials

Display allowances or material are usually used to generate special in-store merchandising activity for a new product or brand extension, but they are also used to stimulate trade support for consumer promotions. The importance of in-store merchandising is underscored by the fact that more than 70 percent of brand choices are made in-store.[13] According to a Gallup study, 56 percent of mass-merchandise shoppers and 62 percent of grocery shoppers said they noticed point-of-purchase material when they were shopping.[14] Figure 5.6 details a number of ways point-of-purchase material is displayed.

According to Standard Rate and Data Service, expenditures for point-of-purchase in 1992 was projected at 15.2 billion dollars, indicating an average growth of 18 percent over the previous decade, and an incredible growth of 57 percent over the last 5 years. This compares to a 5-year growth rate of only a 33 percent increase for magazines, 31 percent increase for radio, 21 percent increase for TV, and 18 percent increase for newspapers according to SRDS.[15]

Figure 5.6
Display Materials for Point-of-Purchase Promotions

- Permanent or temporary signs

- Banners

- Counter cards

- Shelf talkers

- Permanent or temporary display units

- Interactive computers

- In-store television and L.E.D.

Basically, point-of-purchase refers to all those things that are used at the point of sale in order to attract the attention of the customer to the product or service being offered. The objective of point-of-purchase material is to draw attention to a particular brand or product on the shelf or wherever it may be displayed, or to provide information. It should encourage consumers to make an impulse purchase or trial decision, or to learn more about the item being featured. Sometimes it can even guide consumers to other areas of the store for cross-merchandising opportunities. Well designed point-of-purchase frequently acts as a trigger mechanism to remind the consumer of the advertising.

One of the more interesting new applications of point-of-purchase is interactive computer-driven displays. This is a relatively new medium for point-of-purchase (p-o-p), but it is growing in popularity. The consumer interacts with a computer displayed within the p-o-p unit in order to gain information about a product or service. Through the computer the consumer can request a catalog, ask questions, receive data in print-out form, and much more. You find interactive point-of-purchase today at automobile dealerships where they are used to provide shoppers with information about specific models, in retail stores where they are used to access store catalogs, and they are even being introduced in fast-food chains to place orders. The most common applications, however, are where a high-ticket, high-margin purchase is involved, or where a purchasing decision process is more complex.

One of the advantages of using display materials as a trade promotion is that it encourages the trade to actually promote your brand in the store, because the incentive to the retailer is only available upon proof of compliance. It can also usually be quickly implemented, making it a useful tactical tool. The disadvantage is that it does require widespread trade acceptance to be effective, and often must conform to various store guidelines for in-store merchandising.

Trade Premiums and Incentives

Trade premiums and incentives center more upon individual stores or personnel, and as a result are popular with the trade. Premiums offered to the trade are usually in the form of *dealer loaders*. Their goal is much the same as for consumer loading devices; to "load" up the store with product. This is done with some sort of product display where a premium is offered to the consumer, usually as part of the display. For example, a cooler might be offered at a very low price with the purchase of a 12-pack of a soft drink brand.

Incentives are offered to various levels of the trade, and for any number of reasons. Awards or gifts might be offered to individual counter or sales staff at retail for reaching a set level of sales for a brand, to a manager for store sales of a brand, or to staff for devising new or innovative ways of promoting a brand. Incentive programs are an especially good idea for new product introduction or for moving slow products, and they have the advantage of being quick and easy to implement, as well as relatively inexpensive.

The problem with all trade premium and incentive promotions, however, is that many mass merchandisers do not allow them, or have rules that tightly restrict the type of programs acceptable.

Chapter Notes

[1] Rossiter and Percy, *Advertising Communications and Promotion Management.*

[2] This trend is discussed in an article reviewing Donnelly Marketing's 14th annual survey of promotional practices in Karen Herther's "Survey Reveals Implication of Promotion Trends for the '90's," *Marketing News* (March 1, 1993), 7.

[3] A. Krishna, I. S. Currin, and R. W. Shoemaker, "Consumer Perceptions of Promotional Activity," *Journal of Marketing* 55 (1991), 4–16.

[4] K. Herther, "Survey Reveals Implication of Promotion Trends for the '90's," *Marketing News*, March 1, 1993: 7.

[5] L. Loro, "Packaged Goods Expand Database," *Advertising Age*, August 14, 1995: 29.

[6] Herther, "Survey Reveals Implication of Promotion Trends for the '90's."

[7] T. Triplett, "Report of Couponing's Death Has Been Greatly Exaggerated," *Marketing News*, October 10, 1994: 1.

[8] H. Schlossberg, "Coupons Likely to Remain Popular," *Marketing News*, March 29, 1993: 1

[9] T. Triplett, "Meaning behind Contradictory Coupon Figures," *Marketing News*, October 10, 1994: 2.

[10] Ibid.

[11] M. S. Lans, "Legal Hurdles Big Part of Promotion Game," *Marketing News*, October 24, 1994: 15.

[12] These comments were made in a lecture given at Yale University by C. A. Mittelstadt, "The Coming Era of Image-Building Brand Promotions," March 3, 1993.

[13] This information on the incidence of in-store brand choices comes from a consumer buying habits study conducted by the P-O-P Advertising Institute in conjunction with the Meyers Research Center, as reported in *Advertising Age*, October 20, 1995.

[14] Sherman, "Study: Most Shoppers Notice P-O-P Material."

[15] These figures are reported in *Marketing News*, February 1, 1993.

CHAPTER SIX

Direct Marketing and Channels Marketing

In Chapter 7 we will look specifically at media strategy for IMC. But first, there are two areas of marketing communication that are often misunderstood as simply ways of delivering a message rather than a *kind* of message that deserves a look on its own: direct marketing and channels marketing. The first is not new, for direct marketing has been used in one way or another for centuries. Channels marketing, however, is a relatively new idea that combines tactical marketing and traditional co-op advertising. Each may be used with either advertising or promotion, although their primary application has been in the area of promotion.

Direct Marketing Overview

When most people think about direct marketing they think of direct mail. In fact, many marketers assume they are the same. But direct mail is only one part of direct marketing, and while it is a very important part, it is not even the largest in terms of direct marketing dollars. So, there is obviously more to direct marketing than direct mail, but how much more? What makes something direct marketing rather than, say, advertising? Can they be the same thing? Is it really important?

In one sense, it probably doesn't really matter what *you* mean by direct marketing. But as Don Shultz has pointed out,[1] what you mean when you say direct marketing may have absolutely no relationship to what others think is direct marketing. This is always a danger when terms are used loosely, and doubly so in IMC planning. As we shall see as we discuss direct marketing, it is a very specific way of delivering marketing communications, and in that sense may actually be considered more in terms of *media* than as either advertising or promotion. Traditionally, direct marketing was most likely to deal with promotion, but in IMC planning, it should in no way exclude advertising from consideration.

Consumers are unlikely to know or care what marketers call the messages they send, or the way they deliver them, but if we are to be disciplined in our planning, we must care. In fact, consumers think that nearly all the marketing communications they are exposed to are "advertising." This means everything from bumper stickers to coupons to refunds.[2] But if we are to effectively plan IMC programs, there must be agreement upon what we mean by such things as advertising and promotion (as we have already seen in earlier chapters), and what it means to include direct marketing as a part of an IMC program.

What then is direct marketing? According to the Direct Marketing Association, direct marketing is:

> An accountable system of marketing which uses one or more communications media to effect a response. It is an interactive process where responses from or about buyers are recorded in a database for building profiles of potential customers and providing valuable marketing information for more efficient targeting.

Obviously, the Direct Marketing Association has something rather definite in mind, and we shall now look more closely at several components of this definition.

The basic characteristics of direct marketing, following this definition, are that it asks for a behavioral response immediately, and that it can be highly targeted. In fact, it can be aimed at a single individual or a very narrowly defined group of individuals. In addition, every aspect of direct marketing should be tied to a database so statistical analysis can be used to project the effectiveness of any program.

Immediate Response

The point has already been made that *all* forms of marketing communications must address brand awareness, and that even promotion should deal with equity issues via brand attitude objectives. But the primary job of direct marketing is to stimulate the target receiver to take some kind of action *now*—place an order, use a service, or make an inquiry.

Highly Targeted

Since the primary goal of direct marketing is an immediate response, the effort must be highly targeted. We are looking for a single individual or relatively small group of similar people who are likely to respond favorably to our message. Even when mass media are used for direct marketing, an effort is made to target as specific an audience as possible.

Accountability

Accountability is a key issue in direct marketing. While all marketing communication should be cost effective, direct marketing is tightly controlled because of its dependence upon a database. With appropriate models, direct marketing offers the manager not only the opportunity of predicting and measuring responses, but also the ability to determine the actual costs associated with particular responses. Because of the database, one can continually purge and update the files to maximize the cost effectiveness of direct marketing programs.

Jerome Pickholz, chairman and CEO of Ogilvy-Mather Direct, suggests there are two significant hurdles for direct marketing to overcome.[3] The first is building a good database. How does one go about it, and how long does it take? Finding heavy category users is not a particularly difficult job. The problem is that a database must be built over time, and as Pickholz reminds us, this can be a real problem for marketers who are looking for immediate solutions.

The second hurdle is the cost of direct mail. Despite the fact that studies show direct marketing helps to build business, the cost-per-response can seem way out of line. As Pickholz points out: "It's hard for marketers accustomed to a $20 cost per thousand to acclimate themselves to a $500 CPM, no matter how much more effective the medium has proven to be."[4] But the nature of direct marketing does allow for close monitoring of costs, and provides the needed flexibility to evolve increasingly more cost-effective programs.

In any event, a 1994 survey of 100 senior-level marketing decision makers shows that 55 percent expect to be spending *more* in three years on direct marketing (which currently accounts for about 13 percent of their marketing communication budgets).[5]

Difference between Direct Marketing and Advertising

There are a number of ways that direct marketing differs from traditional advertising, and several are detailed in Figure 6.1. Perhaps the most important difference between direct marketing and traditional advertising is that rather than trying to stimulate brand purchase intention through multiple exposures to the message, direct marketing usually has only one attempt to generate a response. The target audience is always asked to do something, and do it now.

Another difference is the personal nature of direct marketing. Because the target audience can be tightly targeted, direct marketing rarely addresses a mass audience. One speaks directly to members of the target audience about their particular needs, and never in the third person.

Distribution is also considered in a much different light. With direct marketing, distribution itself can become an important brand benefit (e.g., "not sold in stores"). Direct marketing also uses the delivery medium (direct mail, telemarketing, broadcast) *as* the marketplace, whereas with traditional advertising distribution is used to define the marketplace. For example, direct marketing is really the only way companies such as Time-Life Books, Columbia House Press, and the Franklin Mint distribute products.

In terms of our communication objectives, we have already pointed out that while both brand awareness and brand attitude must be objectives for all marketing communications, advertising will be more strongly oriented toward brand attitude goals while direct marketing clearly means to stimulate immediate brand purchase intention. Yet just as we saw in Chapter 5 that promotion can and should help support brand equity, direct

---

Figure 6.1
Differences between Direct Marketing and Traditional Advertising

	Direct Marketing	**Traditional Advertising**
Message Delivery	One exposure	Multiple exposures
Brand Benefit	Distribution is an important benefit	Benefits are not channel driven
Distribution	Uses the medium as the marketplace	Uses distribution to define marketplace
Primary Communication Objective	Awareness and brand purchase intention	Awareness and brand attitude
Target Audience	Individual	Mass

marketing too can help build brand equity. In fact, studies conducted by a number of Ogilvy and Mather Direct's clients showed significant positive gains in brand attitudes one to three months after a direct mail campaign.[6]

One final difference is again related to the issue of accountability in direct marketing and databases. In a very real sense direct marketing may be seen as interactive. It takes information about the target audience and directs a message to that audience, which in its turn repays the marketer with new information about the target market, either through a purchase response or request for information. All of this is tracked and measured, providing a record of a program's effectiveness. One of course tracks and measures the effects of advertising, but the accountability is not nearly as tight (although continuous tracking programs for advertising have made significant gains in measuring response to advertising).

When to Use Direct Marketing

Direct marketing can be an important part of IMC planning. But it is important to remember that it is merely *one* way to deliver marketing communication. In today's marketing world it has become an increasingly used tool. It has been reported that the number of direct marketing jobs has doubled in the five-year period since 1990.[7] However, this does not mean that direct marketing need necessarily be a part of any particular IMC campaign, only that it should be considered when appropriate.

Direct marketing is not appropriate for every type of product or service. In fact, it is almost never a good way of marketing most consumer packaged goods products—the kind of products you find in drug stores and supermarkets. While direct marketing can be effective for some low involvement products, its primary use is with high involvement products.

This does not mean that consumer packaged goods marketers do not use marketing communications tools that may look like they are part of a direct marketing campaign. This is where our definition is important. Does the inclusion of an 800-number in advertising constitute direct marketing? Probably not, in most cases. What about direct mail coupons? Again, probably not.

Direct marketing is a way of delivering a message that asks for an immediate response, is highly targeted, and is grounded through a database. In our example, the 800-number is probably a convenience for inquiry, not the primary objective of the marketing communication, and the mass mailing of coupons generally is not highly targeted. When we are considering the use of direct marketing in IMC planning, it should be within the bounds of our definition.

Planning Direct Marketing

There are three questions we must ask when thinking about using direct marketing in an IMC program (see Figure 6.2). First of all: Does direct marketing make sense? As you review the IMC Task Grid, are there situations where a direct response is desirable? Is all or part of your target audience concentrated and easily identifiable? This would certainly be the case, for example, with customers for military aircraft or some specialized manufacturing equipment. But what about consumer markets? As we have mentioned, the key is high involvement.

Again, this does not mean direct marketing is never appropriate for low involvement products. But it does mean that you want to take a closer look if you are marketing low involvement products, and *apply the definition*. Of course too we are assuming these low involvement products are available through traditional mass merchandising chains of distribution. Many catalog and other marketers deal with low involvement products, but direct marketing is their *only* (or primary) means of distribution. These marketers, if they indeed only distribute via direct marketing, do not use IMC.

If direct marketing does make sense, the second question one must ask is: Is a good database available for my target market? If direct marketing has been a part of previous marketing programs, a list is probably available. Many businesses retain customer and prospect lists. If not, lists of businesses and consumers are generally available to rent, covering almost any product category or selected demographic group. If nothing satisfactory is available, consideration could be given to developing custom lists. This, of course would only work if there were time to develop the list.

Figure 6.2
Questions to Answer When Considering Direct Marketing for IMC

- Does direct marketing make sense given my communication objective?
- Is a good database available for the target audience?
- How do I deliver the message?

We will be dealing with the issue of databases in more detail later in this chapter. As our definition implies, a database is required for direct marketing. To underscore the importance of the database in direct marketing, it has been suggested that the quality of the list used accounts for 40 percent of the effectiveness of the direct marketing effort, compared with the headline or primary thrust of the message accounting for another 40 percent, and the remainder of the message only 20 percent.[8] Without a good list, direct marketing is unlikely to be effective.

The last question to ask is: How do I deliver the message? Basically, there are four media to choose from—direct mail, telemarketing, mass media, and interactive media. As a rule, only one form of media will be used in direct marketing when it is part of an IMC program. Other media in the IMC program may play a secondary role by alerting the target market to the direct marketing efforts, but the nature and cost of direct marketing usually dictate a single, primary medium for delivering the message. An exception would be when different segments of the market are more easily reached by one medium over another. Media selections for different direct marketing tasks are highlighted in Figure 6.3, and each of the four major types is discussed next.

Direct Mail

We have already remarked that direct mail and direct marketing are often thought to be merely two ways of saying the same thing. But as we have seen, direct marketing is a *type* of marketing communication, not simply a way of delivering a message. Direct mail is, however, a key medium in direct marketing. It provides the greatest flexibility in targeting audiences, and provides the greatest latitude in creative options. This latter point means direct mail offers the best means of effecting all five communication objectives.

Figure 6.3
Basic Media for Direct Marketing

Direct Mail	greatest flexibility
Telemarketing	provides immediate feedback
Mass Media	more broadly based audience
Interactive Media	largely self-selecting

According to Stone, direct mail has a number of advantages over other direct marketing media:[9]

- As mentioned above, there is greater *selectivity* with direct mail, enabling more precise targeting.

- *Virtually unlimited choice of format* is available with direct mail.

- Direct mail offers a greater ability to *personalize* the message.

- If someone opens and reads a piece of direct mail (a big "if"), there is *no direct competition* for their attention.

- Because you control the mailing dates, whom you mail to, and what you say, direct mail offers *more control.*

- And finally, direct mail offers a *unique capacity to involve the recipient.*

Everything from product samples to corporate gifts, brief postcards to involved messages and catalogs can be delivered via direct mail

Telemarketing

The telephone today probably accounts for the largest amount of direct marketing activity, but not all of that activity would be called telemarketing. Direct marketing requires an immediate response, and the telephone (especially 800-numbers) offers a convenient way of accomplishing this. Telemarketing, however, also implies telephone contact with the target market in order to deliver some kind of message. In a more detailed definition, Stone and Wyman have said that telemarketing:

> comprises the integrated and systematic application of telecommunications and information processing technologies with management systems to optimize the marketing communications mix used by a company to reach its customers. It retains personalized customer interaction while simultaneously attempting to better meet customer needs and improve cost effectiveness.[10]

You can see how closely aligned this definition is with our definition of direct marketing: it enables immediate responses, it can be highly targeted, and it makes use of the best database technologies. It also underscores telemarketing's most positive advantage over other forms of direct marketing: immediate feedback. This is especially helpful in marketing high involvement products because it permits the message to be "customized" to the prospect's concerns and questions as they arise.

Telemarketing does have a potentially significant drawback. By its very nature, it is non-visual. This means if your product requires visual recognition or understanding, telemarketing cannot be used.

Mass Media

Direct marketing can use any mass media, the same media used by traditional advertising and promotion. The fundamental difference is the way in which the media is purchased and used. Direct marketers are looking for media that will deliver the optimum number of *immediate responses* for the least amount of money, and the use of space will be dictated by a different creative style. The use of the four major types of mass media in direct marketing is outlined next.

Television. While in the past direct marketing on television was generally confined to the wee hours of the morning, it is more and more finding its way into prime time. Still not much of a factor in network television, among other reasons because it does not offer precise enough targeting, it is becoming increasingly a part of cable television. One reason for this is the somewhat better targeting potential (e.g., the History Channel, Arts and Entertainment, ESPN, etc.) and the ability to run longer commercials— 60-second, 90-second, and even 2-minute commercials are not uncommon on cable television. The longer commercials, of course, permit more copy, a necessary ingredient when television is used for high involvement products.

Another use of cable television for direct marketing is the "infomercial." These are program length, often 30 minutes long. According to a 1995 survey, the use of infomercials among national brand advertisers is expected to increase significantly in the next few years. In 1994 approximately 13 percent of national brand advertisers produced at least one infomercial, and the number was expected to reach 30 percent by 1997.[11] In fact, there is now a new 24-hour cable channel featuring nothing but infomercials, the Consumer Resource Network. While just beginning, they have already signed up such companies as Ford Motor Company, Schering-Plough, State Farm Insurance, and Fidelity Investments.[12]

Television commercials, and especially longer commercials and infomercials, are a good way to direct market high involvement products where a demonstration is necessary or desirable.

Radio. As might be correctly surmised, radio is not often considered for direct marketing. The obvious reason is the difficulty in effecting an immediate response to the message. Radio is generally a "passive" medium, listened to while driving or engaged in some other activity, making it difficult to switch attention and find pen and paper to write down a telephone number or address in order to respond to the message.

Nevertheless, radio does have the advantage of being able to tightly target specific audiences, and it is relatively economical. It also provides almost instant access for a message. Radio commercials can be quickly produced and aired; even within a day or two if necessary. These are very real advantages, but one must be sensitive to the creative challenge involved in facilitating a response (for example, repetition of an address or telephone number, made easy to remember with, say a mnemonic device).

Newspaper. The primary use of newspapers in direct marketing is for the distribution of various preprinted inserts, principally FSIs (free-standing inserts). The advantage of using newspaper for direct marketing is that almost any length printed message may be inserted, and it does not need to be printed on newsprint stock; almost any paper stock can be used. Another advantage is timeliness. Newspapers are distributed daily, so your message can be scheduled for delivery on any specific day. The disadvantage is that newspapers reach an ever-shrinking market, and circulation is not targeted (except, perhaps, geographically). This means newspaper should only be considered when a broad-based target audience, within specific geographic boundaries, is appropriate.

Magazines. Compared with newspapers, magazines offer the opportunity for rather focused targeting. There are magazines and trade journals aimed at almost any type of audience one might require. Where newspapers utilize FSIs, direct marketing through magazines will use on-page messages in the magazine itself, often with a bound-in postal reply card. There may even be stand-alone cards that by themselves carry the message (known as "blow-ins").

In IMC planning, the inclusion of magazines to deliver direct marketing falls somewhere between highly targeted direct mail that is designed to reach specific audiences and newspapers that deliver a broad-based, geographically targeted audience. The need for specificity of target audience and cost will determine which of the three is most efficient for a printed message.

Interactive Media

Although interactive media play a very small role overall in today's marketing communication programs, there is little doubt that they will grow significantly over the next few years. Technological advances almost guarantee it. Nevertheless, there are serious questions about the extent to which interactive media are likely to ever play a really large role in direct marketing.

According to *Advertising Age*,[13] in 1994 direct marketing received about 13 percent of the marketing budgets of the 100 Leading National Advertisers, while interactive "advertising" accounted for about 3 percent, up from only 1 percent three years previously. Considering that much of this interactive "advertising" is not direct marketing, its potential impact, at least in the near term, is likely to remain small. But we should not ignore the feelings of 98 percent of the senior-level marketing decision makers who participated in the *Advertising Age* study that consumer usage of interactive media will increase over the next five years, and that 75 percent of these marketing executives expect to be spending more on interactive "advertising."

The primary source for access to interactive media is television, and perhaps the earliest example of direct market use was television shopping programs such as the Home Shopping Network. While not technically "interactive," it has certainly conditioned a large number of households to "television shopping," and as CD-ROM-equipped televisions become more common, shopping networks will become truly interactive. For those with CD-ROM-equipped home computers, CD-ROM catalogs are available for interactive shopping (approximately one-quarter of the companies interviewed in the *Advertising Age* study report using them now).

Of course the real star of interactive media for its proponents is the Internet. Again, we advise caution, despite estimates that by the year 2000 some 22 million people will be users of the Internet.[14] There is no question that marketers have rushed to the Internet, including such corporate giants as IBM, J.C. Penney, Hyatt, and Bank of America. Even smaller companies such as Robert Redford's Sundance Catalog are on the Web, and consumer packaged goods marketers such as Coors. But as Harry Rosenthal, president of Sundance Catalog, reminds us, getting people to browse through the catalog isn't the problem, "getting them to buy is hard because they might not be direct response buyers."[15]

This is an important point and brings us back to our definition of direct marketing. We are looking for a highly targeted audience. In one sense, users of the Internet do form a highly targeted market, but only for innovators or computer-oriented people. Otherwise, the market will be self-selecting, and subject to the type of people visiting your Web site.

The Database in Direct Marketing

As our definition of direct marketing implies, a database is at the heart of a direct marketing operation. Before we discuss the database in direct marketing, however, something should be pointed out. Not all uses of a database in marketing constitute direct marketing. In fact, in its broader application, use of databases in marketing is often referred to as "database marketing."

One growing use of database marketing is in the retail area. A study of nearly 300 retailers (including large mass merchandisers such as Sears and J.C. Penney as well as smaller retailers) has revealed that two-thirds currently use database marketing programs, and an additional 40 percent are planning them. They are used for everything from general promotions and information mailings to preventing customer defections and supporting special promotions.[16] Mall marketers too are using database marketing as an aid for their smaller, less sophisticated retailers.[17]

But not all database marketing is direct marketing. And a database is not just another name for a mailing list. A mailing (or telephone) list is indeed essential to a database, but a database is much more. One definition of a database describes it as "a shared collection of interrelated data designed to meet the varied information needs of an organization."[18] This data will generally combine names of customers and prospects (including how to contact them) along with particulars about their buying or usage behavior and other information. Obviously this can be a powerful tool in isolating very specific target groups.

The most effective use of a database is when it is a "closed-loop system," according to the head of a large direct marketing company. In other words one knows "who has been contacted at what time, and at what cost,"[19] and by looking at the costs, evaluate the results. This ensures accountability. It also permits updating and reevaluating the database.

Building a Database

Although it is not essential, if a database is to be truly efficient and cost effective it should be computer based. Direct marketing based upon card files of customers and prospects has been around for a very long time, but obviously much more can be accomplished when access to a database is via computer.

The five steps that go into building and maintaining a database are listed in Figure 6.4. The first step is to *develop a list*. This can be done in any number of ways. If you truly have no customer list, the first step is to

Figure 6.4
Steps in Building a Database

- Develop a list.
- Analyze the list.
- Use the list to implement a direct marketing program.
- Analyze the results of the program.
- Update the list based upon this analysis.

develop one. Regardless, you will want to comb through all available marketing data; you may be surprised what is already on hand. Sales forces keep records, there may be warranty cards, charge records, and so on. If there is time, you could survey your market. A quick start is possible by simply renting or buying a list that corresponds to your target market.

But having a list is not enough. You must *analyze the list*. What information do you have? Do you want to use the entire list? What does the list imply about the type of offer or means of response? Who are customers, who are prospects? Once you understand the content of your database, it is time to *use* it to implement a direct marketing program. Once the program has run, you must *analyze the results*. It is not enough to simply use a database as a source for contacting customers or prospects. You must study the effectiveness of the list. Is there any information in the database that explains why some people may or may not have responded to the message? Here is where computers can really help.

Of course, computers make the last step in developing a database more effective as well. Developing and using a list does not make a database. One must constantly *update* all of the information. Keep track of who does and who does not respond, to what type of messages; what are the purchase rates and patterns; in effect, retain and track the details of every direct marketing program and the response. In a very real sense, you are always building a database.

Effective Use of a Database

Since our definition of direct marketing includes the use of a database, when to use a database in one sense is the same as when one should consider using direct marketing. We have already discussed this. What we want to briefly cover here is how one can use a database to help make direct marketing decisions.

Figure 6.5 outlines four situations in which information in a database can help guide strategic decisions as to whether to include direct marketing in a particular IMC program. The first situation is where we know people on our list make multiple or repeat purchases of our product or service, especially where there are high gross margins. It also helps if the purchase cycle is neither too short nor too long. If the purchase cycle is too short, even if a person is a regular customer, the margin generally will not support specialized direct marketing. If the purchase cycle is too long, unless we know it is time for the customer to repeat, too much of our direct marketing effort would be wasted on people not in the market at the time of the campaign.

A second situation is where specialized niche marketing or segmentation makes sense. Direct marketing is meant to be highly targeted, and a database can reveal important segments. Of course, this assumes we have compiled the relevant information in our database.

Because we know so much about the customers and prospects in our database, it offers unique opportunities for increasing business among them. An obvious example here would be to use the database for cross-selling. Beyond this, by knowing our customers well, it is possible to tailor messages to reduce switching behavior or increase their current usage or purchase of our brand.

Finally, with a good database one can predict when customers are most likely to be in the market, and prevent defections by competitive attempts to lure them away. This is why "quick-lube" outlets send you a reminder card after three months, or a bank reminds you a savings instrument is about to mature.

Analyzing a database with these points in mind will help pinpoint potential direct marketing applications. As one reviews the IMC Task Grid, attention should be paid for opportunities of reaching particular segments that might be suggested by a careful review of your database. If information that might help target particular segments is not in the database, thought should be given to what it might take to add it.

Figure 6.5
Situations a Database Helps Identify for Consideration of Direct Marketing in IMC Planning

---

- Where people who make multiple or repeat purchases are identified
- Where specialized niche marketing or segmentation makes sense
- Where knowledge of our customers offers unique opportunities for increasing business among them
- Predicting when customers will be in the market to prevent defections through competitive promotion

---

Channels Marketing

Channels marketing is a new term that refers to marketing communications geared to assisting the marketer at all levels of trade. The term "channels marketing" has evolved out of the growing importance that we have already noted in trade-oriented promotions. The two principal components of channels marketing are co-op advertising and tactical marketing. While cooperative or co-op advertising has been around for a long time, tactical marketing is something new. Co-op advertising is essentially an arrangement between a marketer and a retailer to cooperate when selling the marketer's brand or service. It consists of advertising programs that are really nothing more than extensions of the marketer's basic marketing communications plan, funded in whole or part by the advertiser and designed to assist the retailer in selling the brand or service.

Tactical marketing, however, is a channel-oriented marketing communication system that is designed to alter the terms of marketing in favor of the manufacturer and leverage incremental support from the trade (particularly retailers) by offering them specific advertising and promotion paid for by the advertiser on an earned basis. Simply put, the concept is to offer the retailer comprehensive customized advertising and promotional support in exchange for incremental sales features, distribution, and/or store space.

While co-op advertising and tactical marketing may appear quite similar, as they should since tactical marketing is an outgrowth of basic co-op principles, the difference lies in the nature of how these techniques are applied. Co-op programs are usually broad in scope and passive in nature. In a typical co-op arrangement, the brand's entire retailer base is eligible to participate, with retailers earning a certain budget for the advertising or promotions based upon sales volume. The manufacturer provides set material for use by the retailer, and then reimburses the retailer for its use on a periodic basis up to the limits of an established budget. Generally the retailers take advantage of the money and marketing communications as they see fit. A manufacturer should make a special attempt to encourage greater retailer participation or a particular strategic shift in retailer activity by manipulating allowances or methods of allocating funds. For the most part, however, traditional co-op programs are fairly straightforward.

Tactical marketing is always a proactive effort. When tactical marketing is considered, the manufacturer is looking for specific and incremental support from a given retailer. In return for this support, the manufacturer will create a specific program tailored to the needs of that retailer, and will fund and implement the program. With tactical marketing the *manufacturer* controls the entire process from beginning to end.

Tactical marketing concepts grew out of the need for brands to provide a more individualized basis than was possible with most co-op programs. In traditional co-op advertising, the manufacturer reimburses the retailers or pays them all or part of the cost of the advertising. As retailers became more and more powerful through consolidation and the formation of buying groups and with the expansion of national chains via mergers, they began using co-op advertising as a profit center to offset their operating costs. Frequently funds went to increasing store margins and other non-advertising functions. With an increasing power advantage, retailers began forcing manufacturers to participate in retailer-initiated programs which may or may not have been to the advantage of the manufacturer or its brands. In effect, the manufacturer had lost control of co-op programs to the retailer.

As a result of this situation, the tactical marketing concept was developed as an alternative retailer marketing system that could provide the manufacturer a means of extending brand support at the retail level with control flexibility, while providing complete coordination and production services to the retailer. This meant that the retailer could take advantage of marketing communications provided by the manufacturer, but in more of a partnership. Tactical marketing also enlarges on the more traditional print orientation of co-op programs by providing the retailer access to television and radio commercials, direct marketing, promotion, sponsorships, outdoor, and other types of IMC activities. But perhaps most importantly in terms of IMC, a specific marketing communications plan customized to particular retailers is utilized.

Overall, while co-op advertising programs tend to be general, passive, and standardized, tactical marketing is specific, proactive, individualized, and highly participatory.

Chapter Notes

[1] D. E. Schultz, "What Is Direct Marketing?" *Journal of Direct Marketing* 9(2) (1995): 5–9.

[2] A study conducted by the Leo Burnett advertising agency indicates that when presented with 100 forms of marketing communications, 94 were called simply "advertising" by consumers surveyed. This included everything from bumper stickers, checkout coupons, refund offers, and FSIs to traditional forms of advertising. This study is reviewed in Schultz, "What Is Direct Marketing?"

[3] J. W. Pickholz, "From the Practitioners," *Journal of Direct Marketing* 8(2) (1994): 2–6.

[4] Ibid.

[5] A. W. Fawatt, "Interactive Looms Large in Budgets," *Advertising Age,* October 3, 1994.

[6] The results of these Ogilvy and Mather direct studies are discussed by J. W. Pickholz in "From the Practitioners."

[7] This data is reported in *Marketing News,* September 25, 1995: 14.

[8] B. Lamons, "Creativity Is Important to Direct Marketers, Too," *Marketing News,* December 7, 1992: 10.

[9] B. Stone, *Successful Direct Marketing Methods,* 3rd ed. (Chicago: Crain Books, 1984), 247–48.

[10] B. Stone and J. Wyman, *Successful Telemarketing* (Lincolnwood, IL: NTC Business Books, 1986), 5.

[11] K. Cleland, "More Advertisers Put Informercials in Their Plan," *Advertising Age,* September 18, 1995: 50.

[12] C. Rubel, "Infomercials Evolve as Major Firms Join Successful Format," *Marketing News,* January 2, 1995: 1.

[13] Fawatt, "Interactive Looms Large in Budgets."

[14] C. Miller, "Marketers Find It's Hip to Be on the Internet," *Marketing News,* February 27, 1995: 2.

[15] Ibid.

[16] K. Shermach, "Large and Small Retailers See Value in Data-base Marketing," *Marketing News,* September 25, 1995: 8.

[17] K. Shermach, "Shopping Malls Becoming Pretty Sophisticated," *Marketing News,* September 25, 1995.

[18] F. R. McFadden and J. A. Hoffer, *Data Base Management* (Menlo Park, CA: Benjamin/Cumming, 1985), 3.

[19] These quotes come from Robert Kestinbaum of Kestinbaum & Company in an editorial in the *Journal of Direct Marketing* 8(3) (1994): 2–3.

CHAPTER SEVEN

Integrating Media Strategy

The job of media is to deliver our message in the most effective way to satisfy the communication objectives of the IMC campaign. Most people think of "media" in terms of traditional advertising: television, radio, newspaper, and magazines. Promotions were rarely thought of in terms of "media." After all, merchandising means in-the-store; direct mail is, well, direct mail. But as we have seen, the distinction between what is advertising and what is promotion has blurred. With IMC planning we must take a broad view of media, and look at media strategy as finding the best way to meet our communication objectives.

The important point here is *not* to think in terms of integrating an advertising media plan and a promotion program, but in terms of developing a plan that considers the best way of accomplishing the communication tasks required. These tasks, of course, are identified in the IMC Task Grid that summarizes the Communication Strategy Worksheets and Behavioral Sequence Model (the planning tools introduced in Chapter 3). Looking at media strategy in this way ensures we are thinking about media in terms of how *consumers* think and behave.

You will recall that the first two considerations in the BSM provide a timeline showing the likely steps involved in the purchase decision process and those who are involved. At a macro level this tells us how to begin thinking about possible media alternatives. The full BSM tells us how to get our message to consumers when and where it counts. This echoes Schultz's point that "the real question is how to integrate (media) from the view of the consumer."[1]

Since we view "media" as the means of delivering our message to the target market in order to satisfy communication objectives, our perspective must include these objectives. This means we will be looking at IMC media strategy in terms of the two communication objectives necessary for all marketing communication: brand awareness and brand attitude. First, we will want to look more generally at how we select media within our choices of advertising and/or specific promotions.

Selecting Appropriate Media for Marketing Communications

The IMC Task Grid helped us identify whom we wanted to reach in our target market and with what type of marketing communications in order to meet our communication objective. You will also remember that we talked about the need to determine a primary communication task, and the best way of accomplishing that task, in order to develop a "lead" creative brief.

This all bears significantly upon IMC media strategy. For example, if the primary communication task is best satisfied by a highly targeted message through direct mail, that becomes the thrust of the media strategy. Media for other parts of the IMC campaign will then be looked at either in support of that message or to cover secondary communication tasks; and only after adequate money is allocated for the direct mail program.

While mass media advertising is often the best way to satisfy many primary communication tasks, when it is not the best solution, it is unlikely to figure in the media strategy at all. Of course, this is not a hard-and-fast rule, but it is a good rule of thumb. The reason for this lies in the general reach objectives of advertising and promotion. As we have seen, most of the time promotions are aimed at a more highly targeted audience or a narrow reach. Given the broad-based reach of mass media advertising, it is unlikely to be efficient in support of a more narrowly based target audience.

Yet as we know, and shall discuss in some detail below, many promotions simply are not very efficient without corresponding or prior advertising support. This can be a real problem. But this support can come from such media as specialized print media, local radio, and cable television that can be adapted to more targeted audiences and narrower reach, rather than by traditional "mass" media. When broad-based mass markets are not the target for your primary communication task, for effective IMC planning you must begin to think of traditional advertising media in a more narrow way.

Advertising-Oriented Media

While almost any medium can serve as a means of delivering an advertising message, those traditionally considered as mass media are television, radio, newspapers, and magazines. As we shall see when we look at the effectiveness of individual media in meeting brand awareness and brand attitude communication objectives, as a group, mass advertising media tend to be more effective than promotion media for satisfying brand awareness objectives. But interestingly, promotion media do a better job overall in satisfying brand attitude objectives. This is surprising because the strength of advertising is brand attitude. The answer to this seeming contradiction is that it is promotion *media*, not the promotions themselves that offer this overall advantage. But of course, most promotion media are not mass media, and so not appropriate for broad-based advertising.

In fact, the *best* overall medium, period, is television. It is the best way for achieving any of the five communication objectives. Also, in study after study, when television is compared with other mass media such as radio or magazines, messages delivered by television do a better job driving sales.

There are several reasons for this. To begin with, television employs words and pictures, movement and sounds. Radio offers words and sound, but no pictures or movement. Magazines offer words and pictures, but no movement or sound. Television offers high reach, and can combine it with high effective frequency. This is very difficult for either radio or magazines. Newspapers generally have the same problems as magazines.

Does this mean we should only be considering television when selecting a mass medium for advertising? The general answer is "yes." However, as we know, for many reasons television may not be a viable choice. Nevertheless, when possible, television should be the medium of choice for mass advertising except for high involvement, informational strategies. We will look more closely at these strategic considerations later in this chapter.

Promotion-Oriented Media

Are there such things as promotion media? Of course, only we usually don't think about them in terms of media. But in IMC planning it is important to think of each way our advertising message or promotion can be delivered as a medium within the overall media strategy. We will consider promotion media to include mass media (as a group), direct mail,

FSIs, and point-of-purchase. Again, each of these vehicles could be (and often are) used to deliver an advertising message, but with the exception of mass media, the others are primarily means of delivering a promotion.

The most likely promotion media choice for each of the six consumer promotions are shown in Figure 7.1, and discussed next.

Refunds and Rebates. The primary medium for a refund or rebate promotion is mass media. The reason for this is that refunds and rebates must be announced and explained. This is ideally accommodated within an advertising message. The next most likely means of handling a refund or rebate would be at the point of purchase or through an FSI.

Sampling. The two best ways of delivering samples are at the point of purchase or with direct mail. Sampling in-store or at a central location is perhaps the least expensive way of sampling, and for many products, it is the only effective way. Direct mail is somewhat limited by the type of sample one can mail, but with a good mailing list it has the advantage of being able to better target delivery.

Figure 7.1
Primary Promotion Media for the Six Basic Consumer Promotions

CONSUMER PROMOTION	PROMOTION MEDIA
Refunds and rebates	mass media
	p-o-p
	FSIs
Sampling	p-o-p
	direct mail
Loyalty and loading devices	direct mail
	p-o-p
	mass media
Coupons	direct mail
	FSIs
	p-o-p
Premiums	mass media
	direct mail
	p-o-p
Sweepstakes, games, and contests	mass media
	direct media
	p-o-p

Loyalty and Loading Devices. Depending upon the specific promotion, direct mail or point-of-purchase are the most likely media for a loyalty or loading promotion. Loyalty programs are perhaps best suited to direct mail, while most loading promotions are best delivered at the point of purchase. While loyalty and loading devices do not necessarily require advertising, it is often useful to include mass media announcements or explanations of the program, especially if they are aimed at a broad-based audience.

Coupons. There are many ways of delivering coupons, but the most effective are direct mail and free-standing inserts. Direct mail offers greater flexibility in targeting, but FSIs are about half the cost. Coupons may also be offered at the point of purchase, and as we mentioned when we discussed coupons in Chapter 5, coupons may now be offered electronically through on-line services.

Premiums. Much like refunds or rebates, to be successful a premium promotion will generally require mass media advertising to generate awareness and interest. This is especially true if the premium is aimed at a broad-based audience. More narrowly targeted premium promotions utilize direct mail or point-of-purchase. Regardless of the primary medium, any premium promotion will also want to utilize in-store merchandising.

Sweepstakes, Games, and Contests. In sweepstakes, games, and contests we again have a situation where mass media is required to announce and explain the promotion, unless it is aimed at a more targeted audience where direct mail will work. Also, as with premiums, point-of-purchase display will be needed.

Matching Communication Objectives to Media Selection

In Chapter 2 we discussed the importance of brand awareness and brand attitude communication objectives for all marketing communication. We must also consider these objectives when selecting media because individual marketing communication mediums vary in their ability to facilitate meeting these communication objectives.

Looking at these two basic communication objectives, there are three important considerations bearing upon media selection. For brand awareness, is it necessary to *see* the package? For brand attitude, how much *time* is necessary for processing? For both, how much *frequency* is required to effectively communicate? Figure 7.2 summarizes these requirements for recognition versus recall brand awareness, and for each of the four brand attitude strategies. If our objective is recognition awareness, the media selected must have the ability to show the package. If recall awareness is our objective it is not necessary to see the package, but the media must be able to deliver high frequency in order to seat the brand–category need link in the target audience's mind.

You will remember that the Rossiter-Percy grid identifies four strategic quadrants defining brand attitude communication effect: low involvement/informational, low involvement/transformational, high involvement/informational, and high involvement/transformational. These four brand attitude strategies result from considerations of the risk involved in the purchase or usage decision, and whether or not the motivations that drive the decision are negative or positive. In terms of media selection, as a general rule when dealing with negative motives, the informational strategies, it is not necessary to provide visual content. However, it is necessary for transformational strategies. This is true regardless of involvement. High involvement/informational strategies require media that provide an opportunity for longer processing (e.g., print media); and low involvement/transformational strategies require media that can provide a high frequency.

Figure 7.2

Media Requirements for the Essential Communication Objectives of Brand Awareness and Brand Attitude

	MEDIA REQUIREMENT		
COMMUNICATION OBJECTIVES	**Visual Content**	**Time to Process**	**Frequency**
Brand Awareness			
recognition awareness	yes	short	low
recall awareness	no	short	high
Brand Attitude			
low involvement/informational	no	short	low
low involvement/transformational	yes	short	high
high involvement/informational	no	long	low
high involvement/transformational	yes	short	low

Source: Adapted from Rossiter and Percy, 1997.

Now that we have reviewed the overall requirements in selecting specific media for an IMC program to satisfy the two critical communication objectives, we shall discuss specific advertising and promotion media in terms of their ability to meet these objectives.

Selecting Advertising Media

When advertising messages are part of our IMC programs, we generally have a choice of television, radio, newspaper, or magazines. Of course, we could use direct mail, outdoor, or many other media, but for our purposes we will be discussing only these four. For any medium not considered here or in the discussion of promotion media in the next section, you need only consider whether it does or does not satisfy the general media requirements for the particular aspect of the communication objective that applies, as outlined in Figure 7.2.

Satisfying the Brand Awareness Communication Objective

When our brand awareness objective is *recognition*, all of the traditional advertising media work, with the obvious exception of radio. One must also be careful when using newspaper for brand recognition if correct color is important in recognizing the brand at the point of purchase. Often four-color advertising is not available, and even when it is, the quality of reproduction frequently leaves much to be desired. On the other hand, when brand *recall* is our objective, all of the traditional advertising media may be used. The only potential concern would be the frequency potential of magazines. A key here is the purchase cycle of your product or service. The longer the purchase cycle, the less of a problem lower-frequency magazines pose. (See Figure 7.3.)

Satisfying the Brand Attitude Communication Objective

If a low involvement/informational brand attitude strategy is called for, any of the four traditional advertising media can do the job. The only possible concern here is that if you must demonstrate your product or service in order to communicate the benefit claim effectively, then it may be difficult to use radio or print.

For low involvement/transformational brand attitude strategies, we must be more selective. Television is the best medium; the others all have potential limitations. Radio is limited because the visual content is essential for two of the three positive motives that are associated with this brand attitude strategy. If the motive involved is intellectual stimulation, visual content in the advertising is not critical, but for both sensory gratification and social approval it is. Try to imagine food or glamour without a picture! A really great creative execution might just manage it, but the odds are against you. Newspapers and magazines suffer from the same potential problem here that we saw with recall brand awareness. The visual quality of color in newspaper, when available, could be a problem. For example, if you want to show a really delicious-looking plate of food, the color must be perfect. Since low involvement/transformational messages require a higher frequency to effectively communicate, the lower frequency of magazines can be a problem.

High involvement/informational brand attitude strategies are easily met with newspapers and magazines, but broadcast media can pose a problem. The key here is the requirement of enough time to process the message. Obviously readers of newspapers and magazines have the ability to control their rate of exposure, taking as much time as they desire to process the message. With television and radio, however, there may not be enough time to process the more detailed messages required for high involvement/informational brand attitude. However, television could become more viable (especially cable television) if longer commercials or infomercials are feasible.

When high involvement/transformational brand attitude strategies are required, most traditional advertising media may be used. But just as we noted with low involvement/transformational strategies, we know that visual content will be necessary when dealing with sensory gratification or social approval motives. This means that color could be a problem with newspapers, and that radio would only be appropriate for high involvement products or services where intellectual stimulation is the motive. (See Figure 7.4.)

Selecting Promotion Media

When promotions are part of our IMC program, we generally have a choice of mass media, direct mail, FSIs, and point-of-purchase, as we have already seen. Once again, however, we must remember that there are certainly other media that may be considered for delivering a promotion message (for example, sponsorships and event marketing). When such media suggest themselves, their appropriateness must be judged in relationship to the requirements necessary for effectively dealing with the communication objective involved, as outlined in Figure 7.2.

If mass media is to be used for a promotion, selection should be made following the same guidelines just discussed for advertising. Here we will consider the suitability of direct mail, FSIs, and point-of-purchase for each of the critical brand awareness and brand attitude communication objectives.

Satisfying the Brand Awareness Communication Objective

One of the problems with these three promotion media when the objective is recognition brand awareness is that almost always some sort of prior exposure to the brand will be necessary before it can be recognized in the mailing, insert, or at the point-of-purchase. Remember that with most frequently purchased consumer products, the potential buyer sees and recognizes the brand, and that recognition reminds him or her of the need. Without some kind of prior knowledge of the brand, usually through advertising, the brand will not be recognized. If the brand is not recognized, the promotion is unlikely to work.

This is really a very important point, and underscores the need for careful IMC planning. Most coupon promotions, for example, are for just such frequently purchased consumer products, products that are bought via brand recognition awareness. While a well-known brand name that has not advertised for some time might have enough residual brand recognition to use such promotion media alone, less well-known brands, and especially new products or brands, cannot. This seems to have been the strategy of Heinz in the mid 1990s. They made a decision to promote without any advertising, and primarily in promotion media. But even with such a well-known brand, one must seriously question how effective such a strategy will be in the long term, especially if competitors continue to advertise. Eventually, one would expect the competitor brands to capture a larger and larger share of the consumer's mind, and be more readily recognized, and as a result more likely to trigger need and purchase.

While these are broader strategic issues, they nonetheless show how important it is to consider the appropriateness of specific media for particular communication objectives.

Looking at recall brand awareness, we are confronted with the same kind of problem. Recall brand awareness occurs in response to a need. The need occurs, and the consumer remembers or "recalls" a brand that will satisfy that need. Unfortunately, the very nature of promotion media, as we saw with recognition awareness, makes it difficult to build the necessary foundation for brand awareness without previous brand exposure. The problem with point-of-purchase is precisely that it is at the point-of-purchase and as a result cannot stimulate brand recall prior to a store visit. It was when the need occurred, prior to the store visit, that a brand was recalled to meet the need. Both FSIs and direct mail are also limited by their low frequency. Recall awareness requires high frequency in order to establish the link between category need and brand awareness.

What we see here is that, other than mass media, most promotion media are limited across the board in terms of their ability to facilitate either recognition or recall brand awareness. This does not mean they are unsuitable, only that they are limited in satisfying the brand awareness communication objective. The suitability of both advertising-oriented (mass media) and promotion-oriented media for the brand awareness communication objective is summarized in Figure 7.3.

This potential problem with awareness underscores how IMC planning can really help. Direct mail, FSIs, and point-of-purchase are frequently the best media for delivering promotions; that is, better than mass media.

Figure 7.3
Media Appropriateness for Brand Awareness Communication Objective

	BRAND AWARENESS COMMUNICATION OBJECTIVE	
MEDIA	**RECOGNITION**	**RECALL**
Advertising Oriented		
television	Yes	Yes
radio	No	Yes
newspaper	visual content limitation	Yes
magazines	Yes	frequency limitation
Promotion Oriented		
direct mail	limited[1]	frequency limitation
FSIs	limited[1]	frequency limitation
point-of-purchase	limited[1]	No

[1]Limited because to be effective requires prior exposure to the brand
Source: Adapted from Rossiter and Percy, 1997.

But without mass media in some capacity to build a foundation of brand awareness, promotions alone in such media are unlikely to be effective. This means that some form of mass media (television, radio, newspaper, or magazine) will almost always be required as the primary medium for an IMC program, even when a major part of a campaign is promotion.

Yet isn't direct mail often used by itself? Of course, but as a rule within a *direct marketing* program that includes other marketing communications (as we shall discuss directly), not as a way of independently delivering either an advertising-oriented message or promotion. This may seem confusing, since direct mail frequently seems to be doing just that. However, if one looks closely at direct mail, when it is well executed it will be part of a direct marketing program or part of a broader IMC program that includes mass media to support brand awareness. The next time you receive a packet of coupons and other promotions in the mail, notice which ones catch your attention. They will be familiar brands! If there is no prior exposure to the brand, that marketer is wasting its money.

Satisfying the Brand Attitude Communication Objective

We remarked earlier on the seeming efficiency of promotion media such as direct mail, FSIs, and point-of-purchase over advertising media in dealing with brand attitude communication objectives. In terms of the requirement of visual content, time to process, and frequency this is certainly true. As a result this should and does facilitate the potential for building brand equity through well-executed promotion material.

Continuing to focus on these three promotion media, we find that all three satisfy the requirements for low involvement/informational brand attitude strategies. Remembering that this was also true for mass media, it means that any medium will be acceptable for delivering promotions within a low involvement/informational brand strategy.

While there were some limitations with print mass media, there are none with the three promotion media for low involvement/transformational brand attitude strategies. This means that, with the exception of some potential limits with newspapers and magazines when dealing with positively motivated behavior, any of the media we are considering meet the selection requirements for low involvement product or service decisions.

When we consider high involvement/informational brand attitude strategies we find that there may be a potential problem with some point-of-purchase material owing to the longer processing time required by the more involved messages needed to gain acceptance of the promotion message. There should be no problem with either direct mail or FSIs. The only media unacceptable for high involvement/informational promotions would be mass media broadcast, as we noted earlier for advertising messages. The problem here, as with point-of-purchase, is the likely lack of time for extended processing. A possible exception, of course, would be longer infomercials used to present the promotion.

The only potential problem in selecting promotion media for high involvement/transformational brand attitude strategies would lie with newspapers and radio because of their visual content limitations (which were detailed when they were discussed as advertising media). Of mass media, television and magazines meet our requirements for high involvement/ transformational strategies, as do direct mail, FSIs, and point-of-purchase.

To help you better understand all of this, Figure 7.4 summarizes how each of the advertising-oriented (mass media) and promotion-oriented media satisfy the requirements for brand attitude communication objectives.

Figure 7.4
Media Appropriateness for Brand Attitude Communication Objectives

MEDIA	BRAND ATTITUDE COMMUNICATION OBJECTIVE			
	Low involvement/ Informational	Low involvement/ Transformational	High involvement/ Informational	High involvement/ Transformational
Advertising Oriented				
television	Yes	Yes	No	Yes
radio	Yes	visual content limitation	No	visual content limitation
newspaper	Yes	visual content limitation	Yes	visual content limitation
magazines	Yes	frequency limitation	Yes	Yes
Promotion Oriented				
direct mail	Yes	Yes	Yes	Yes
FSIs	Yes	Yes	Yes	Yes
point-of-purchase	Yes	Yes	time to process limitation	Yes

Source: Adapted from Rossiter and Percy, 1997.

Selecting Direct Marketing Media

In Chapter 6 when we introduced direct marketing, we talked in a general way about the four major types of media used in direct marketing: mass media, direct mail, telemarketing, and interactive media. If direct mail is used when direct marketing is part of an IMC program, selection should be made following the same guidelines just discussed for selecting direct mail as a promotion media. However, when mass media is considered, we must look at it differently from how we view it for advertising or promotion messages. We will discuss this, along with the suitability of telemarketing and interactive media for both brand awareness and brand attitude communication objectives.

Satisfying the Brand Awareness Communication Objective

As we know from our discussion of direct marketing, it requires an immediate response. For this reason it is very difficult for direct marketing media to satisfy brand awareness communication objectives on their own. (Of course, direct marketing is often used without a brand awareness objective when direct marketing is the only means of marketing the product, but we are not considering this.) When the brand awareness objective is recognition, this means the potential purchaser or user must recognize the brand at the time a decision to purchase is made. For new products or services, it would be impossible to simply use direct marketing; there would be no prior awareness of the product to recognize. For existing products or services, as long as there has been sufficient prior exposure to the brand through other IMC media, direct marketing media can work. One exception would be radio, which would only work if the brand recognition was verbal, for example with insurance companies.

We have a different problem when the brand awareness objective is recall. We know that recall awareness requires more than one exposure, but with direct marketing we are looking for an immediate response. This limits mass media and direct mail, and quite eliminates telemarketing and interactive. The frequency with which direct marketing messages would have been seen or heard prior to the decision is simply too low to be effective. Remember, with recall awareness it is the category need that triggers the awareness. So to work at all, at least in terms of awareness, some other advertising or promotion must have seeded the category need–brand awareness link.

While direct marketing does not do a good job meeting brand awareness communication objectives, it certainly can work because, as we shall see next, it does satisfy brand attitude communication objectives. But only, as should now be clear, if there has been some prior exposure to the brand. There may be exceptions, especially for low involvement decisions, but a good IMC program would not utilize direct marketing on its own without prior brand exposure. The appropriateness of direct marketing media in satisfying brand awareness communication objectives is summarized in Figure 7.5.

Satisfying the Brand Attitude Communication Objective

With only a few exceptions, direct marketing media do a good job of satisfying all of the brand attitude communication objectives. Mass media perform generally the same for direct marketing as they do for advertising and promotion. A significant exception is television. You will remember that television is not an appropriate medium for high involvement/infor-

---

Figure 7.5

Media Appropriateness for Brand Awareness Communication Objective When Using Direct Marketing

| | BRAND AWARENESS COMMUNICATION OBJECTIVE | |
MEDIA	RECOGNITION	RECALL
Mass Media		
television	limited[1]	frequency limitation
radio	No	frequency limitation
newspaper	limited[1]	frequency limitation
magazines	limited[1]	frequency limitation
Direct mail	limited[1]	frequency limitation
Telemarketing	No	No
Interactive	limited[1]	No

[1]Limited because to be effective requires prior exposure to the brand
Source: Adapted from Rossiter and Percy, 1997.

mational advertising because of the short commercial length. With 15-second or 30-second commercials it is difficult if not impossible to provide enough information to convince. But with direct marketing much longer commercials are used; everything from 90-second or 2-minute commercials to 15-minute or 30-minute "infomercials." As a result, television can be used for high involvement/informational messages in direct marketing; and for the same reason, radio can be used as well.

The only limitations we must be concerned with when using mass media for direct marketing are the lack of visual content with radio and potential color problems with newspaper, when our brand attitude communication objective is transformational and based upon either sensory gratification or social approval motives. This is the same limitation we saw for advertising and promotion.

Both direct mail and interactive media are appropriate for any brand attitude objective, but telemarketing suffers from the same visual content limitation as radio. With transformational strategies resulting from sensory gratification or social approval motivations, telemarketing is inappropriate. Again, however, just as we have seen for radio, if the transformational message addresses the third positive motive of intellectual stimulation, telemarketing would be appropriate.

The appropriateness of direct marketing media for the various brand attitude communication objectives is summarized in Figure 7.6.

Minimum Effective Frequency

A review of basic media planning is beyond the scope of this book. We assume the reader understands the basic concepts of reach and frequency, and the trade-offs required in building a media plan. However, there is one aspect of media planning that we feel is not generally well understood, and which is important to media selection, especially for IMC programs. This is the notion of *minimum effective frequency*.

How often must our target audience be exposed to ensure effective message delivery? This is not an easy question, and it certainly is not answered by the misunderstood "3+" notion that seems to have become part of media "wisdom" over the years (or even the newly touted "2+").[2] There really is no single answer to this question. But, one must nonetheless deal with the problem. We recommend a system of estimation developed by Rossiter and Percy[3] based upon a general understanding of how various media are used.

Figure 7.6
Media Appropriateness for Brand Attitude Communication Objective When Using Direct Marketing

MEDIA	BRAND ATTITUDE COMMUNICATION OBJECTIVE			
	Low involvement/ Informational	Low involvement/ Transformational	High involvement/ Informational	High involvement/ Transformational
Mass Media				
television	Yes	Yes	Yes	Yes
radio	Yes	visual content limitation	Yes	visual content limitation
newspaper	Yes	visual content limitation	Yes	visual content limitation
magazines	Yes	Yes	Yes	Yes
Direct Mail	Yes	Yes	Yes	Yes
Telemarketing	Yes	visual content limitation	Yes	visual content limitation
Interactive	Yes	Yes	Yes	Yes

Source: Adapted from Rossiter and Percy, 1997

In their approach, they address the likely effect of whom a message is directed toward and the objectives of that communication upon how it will be received. This fits quite well with how we have been looking at IMC planning. Beginning with the assumption that at least one exposure will be necessary within each purchase cycle for frequently purchased products and services, or some other reasonable advertising or promotion period for less frequently purchased products or services, additional exposures are considered according to four factors: attention value of the selected media, target audience, communication objectives, and the extent that personal influence is involved.

Depending upon the communication task, the minimum effective frequency (MEF) required may be established with the following formula:[4]

$$MEF = 1 + VA(1,2)[TA + BA + BATT - PI]$$
where
MEF = minimum effective frequency
VA(1,2) = vehicle attention factor (either 1 for high-attention vehicles or 2 for low-attention vehicles)

TA = target audience
BA = brand awareness objective
BATT = brand attitude objective
PI = effect of personal involvement

In effect, the MEF estimation depends first upon whether or not the media vehicle considered for delivering the communication is a high- or low-attention vehicle. If a high-attention vehicle is being considered (those would include such things as prime-time TV and daytime soaps, primary print readers, and direct mail), there is no correction factor applied. If a low-attention vehicle is considered, the resulting value of combining the other factors will be doubled. Secondly, the estimate will depend upon specific correction factors related to the remaining variables. These corrective factors are briefly described next.

MEF Correction Factors

Target Audience. Depending upon the composition of our target audience, we might expect differences in what they will want or need to know about our product or service. For example, current brand users should be easier to communicate with than non-users. Rossiter and Percy suggest no correction factor for brand loyals, adding 1 more exposure for brand switchers who use our brand and 2 for those who don't. Dealing with new category users is a bit more difficult, and something we shall leave for the interested reader to pursue on their own in Rossiter and Percy's *Advertising Communications and Promotion Management.*[5]

Brand Awareness. You will remember that brand awareness, along with brand attitude, is always a communication objective. When the brand awareness objective is recognition, because the communication task is relatively easy, no additional exposures are required. On the other hand, recall brand awareness requires multiple exposures to firmly set the link between category need and the brand. What Rossiter and Percy suggest here is to use a correction factor equal to the frequency currently used by your largest competitor plus 1, or to add 2 if yours is the largest brand.

Brand Attitude. Here we are only concerned with the underlying motive. The involvement dimension of brand attitude is assumed to be covered by the target audience factor. We know that informational brand strategies are easily communicated, so no correction factor is needed. Transformational brand strategies, on the other hand, require a great deal of repetition.

As with recall brand awareness, Rossiter and Percy recommend adding a corrective factor equal to the largest competitor plus 1, or 2 if you are the largest brand.

An important point here is that if we are dealing with recall brand awareness and transformational brand attitude strategies, the leading competitor exposure level is only added once, but the "plus 1" would be counted twice. In other words, in this case the BA correction factor would be the exposure level of the leading competitor plus 1, and the BATT correction factor only a plus 1. If you are the leading brand, BA would be a plus 2 and BATT would be plus 2.

Personal Influences. The last potential correction factor deals with the extent to which *nonmarketing* communication may play a part in enhancing brand awareness and brand attitude. This is what is usually called "word of mouth," but one must be careful here. It is not unusual for an advertisement to stimulate positive talk, but it may not be among your target audience; or it may not be associated with the advertised brand. If you really believe there is significant positive word-of-mouth for your product or service, when estimating MEF, subtract 1 exposure from the sum of the target audience and communication objective corrections.

You should now have a good idea of how the correction factors build upon the absolute minimum of one exposure. Starting with one exposure, you add up any corrections required because of your target audience brand awareness and brand attitude communication objective, subtract one exposure if a lot of personal influence is involved with the brand. Then, if the medium considered is high attention, simply add this total to 1 for the MEF required. If a low-attention vehicle is involved, double the total and add it to 1 for the MEF estimate. These correction factors are summarized in Figure 7.7.

We have introduced this concept of minimum effective frequency because it underscores how all of the theory we have been talking about relates to every aspect of IMC planning. Media strategy is not independent of the strategic thinking that went into developing the IMC plan. In the first part of this chapter we saw how important communication objectives are in the selection of appropriate advertising or promotion media. Now we have seen that they affect scheduling as well.

MEF and Promotion Media

From our introduction to estimating MEF, its application to advertising media should be obvious. But what of promotion media? Does the MEF formula also apply when using point-of-purchase, FSIs, and direct mail; and to mass media when used for promotion? While the answer is "yes," estimating the MEF needed when promotion media are being considered is not as straightforward as it is for advertising media. To begin with, by its very nature the MEF when using point-of-purchase will always be 1. But with mass media, FSIs, and direct mail, we must take another look at the correction factors in light of the communication objectives for promotions.

The first question to ask yourself is how important will the brand equity aspect of the promotion be. The more important it is, the more likely it will be that brand attitude will be an important communication

---

Figure 7.7
Corrections Required for Estimating Minimum Effective Frequency

---

CORRECTION FACTOR	CORRECTION REQUIRED
Vehicle Attention	
high	None
low	Double target audience, communication objectives and personal influence total
Target Audience	
brand loyal	None
switch, but use brand	Add 1 exposure
non-users	Add 2 exposures
Communication Objective	
recognition brand awareness	None
recall brand awareness	Add 1 exposure plus exposure level of leading brand, or 2 if you are leading brand
informational brand attitude	None
transformational brand attitude	Add 1 exposure plus exposure level of leading brand, or 2 if you are leading brand
Personal Influence	
insignificant	None
significant	Subtract 1 exposure

Source: Adapted from Rossiter and Percy, 1997

objective for the promotion. With more short-term tactical promotions, such as coupons, the brand equity component will be less important, and brand attitude will be secondary to brand purchase intention as a communication objective. If building or sustaining brand equity is an important part of the promotion, MEF should be estimated with the formula as already discussed. But more often than not brand equity will not be a primary consideration with a promotion, and then we must take another look at the correction factors in the MEF equation. In that case, the correction factors should be applied as follows:

Vehicle Attention. If mass media is to be used for delivering the promotion, the attention values are the same as they would be for advertising, just as they were discussed. When using either FSIs or direct mail, the attention value is high so *no* correction is required.

Target Audience. With the exception of loyalty programs, most promotions are aimed either at brand switchers or non-users of the brand. This means that an additional exposure is needed for brand switchers or two additional exposures if the target audience includes those loyal to another brand.

Brand Awareness and Brand Attitude. Both brand awareness and brand attitude should be set at zero. While it is true that brand awareness and brand attitude are always communication objectives for promotions, when brand equity is not a significant part of the promotion, both brand awareness and brand attitude will be secondary communication objectives. You will also remember that there are potential problems with both FSIs and direct mail when the brand awareness objective is recall, because of frequency limitations.

Personal Influence. If you feel a particular promotion will excite a great deal of comment and interest, this could certainly influence attention to the promotion and mediate the need for the extra exposure or two required by the target audience. So when appropriate, one less exposure would be needed.

To summarize all of this, MEF when using promotion media will generally be lower than the MEF required when using advertising media. The MEF for point-of-purchase will always be 1. For high involvement mass media vehicles, FSIs, and direct mail, the MEF will be 1 or 2 for switchers and 2 or 3 for other-brand loyals, depending upon whether or not there is likely to be a strong personal influence. Only when a low-attention mass media vehicle is being considered will the MEF be larger than this, and then just double these levels: 2 or 4 for switchers and 4 or 6 for other-brand loyals.

The reason for these lower MEF estimates when using promotion media is owing to the basic difference between promotion-oriented and advertising-oriented messages. The primary communication objective of advertising is almost always brand awareness and brand attitude, and these factors must be considered when estimating MEF. The primary communication objective for promotion is almost always brand purchase intention, so we are not concerned with possible corrections for brand awareness and brand attitude in our MEF estimates.

The IMC Media Budget Allocation Grid

We should now have a good idea of what media to select in order to satisfy our primary brand awareness and brand attitude communication objective. Also, with our formula for estimating minimum effective frequency, we have a good idea of what it will take to effectively meet our communication objectives with the media we have selected. Now it is time to put together an IMC media plan.

While it is beyond the scope of this book to get into the details of media planning, we would like to offer one last planning grid to help visualize the allocation of IMC media dollars. Back in Chapter 3 we introduced a series of planning tools that help summarize and focus our thinking as we consider the various communication options available to us for positively affecting purchase and usage decisions. These culminated in the IMC Task Grid (see Figure 3.11). In Chapter 4 we discussed the various strengths and weaknesses of traditional advertising versus promotion, and the need to determine whether advertising or promotion should be the primary focus of any particular IMC campaign.

All of this will help us as we begin to strategically look at an integrated media plan. Figure 7.8 introduces an IMC Media Budget Allocation Grid. What it does is bring together the various communication tasks that are to be accomplished and the various IMC options that will be needed to get the job done. This information comes directly from the IMC Task Grid. It also asks for the primary versus secondary IMC options. As we learned in Chapter 4, this will generally be a simple advertising versus promotion decision, but *any* combination of IMC tools may be considered primary versus secondary.

Figure 7.8
IMC Media Budget Allocation Grid

IMC Communication Options	Communication Tasks				
Primary:					
Secondary:					

To gain some idea of how the IMC Media Budget Allocation Grid can be used, let us return to the cruise vacation example discussed in Chapter 3. Figure 3.9 illustrated a hypothesized BSM for a Cruise Vacation. Using this information one might construct an IMC Task Grid similar to the one shown in Figure 7.9. From the BSM we have developed specific communication tasks for each decision stage (along the lines of the relationships between decision stage, communication effects, and communication tasks shown in Figure 3.10), isolated target audiences, speculated upon the best place to reach them, and identified the IMC options likely to be most effective.

Specifically, we can see that during the early need arousal stage of the decision process, we are assuming that for our target audience there is at least some latent interest in cruise vacations. This means we do not need to be concerned with stimulating interest in the category (cruising). The communication tasks early in the decision process are to stimulate awareness of our cruise line in response to any interest in cruising, along with a tentatively positive attitude toward our cruise line. This early communication is to be aimed at people who have cruised before, and those interested in cruising. At the same time, we must also be addressing these same messages to travel agents, not as potential cruisers, but as potential initiators and influencers. In order to accomplish these communication tasks we have selected broadcast advertising to drive up awareness and begin to build a positive brand attitude among potential cruisers, along with direct mail to known cruise and travel agents.

Figure 7.9
IMC Task Grid for Cruise Vacation

Decison Stage	Communication Task	Target Audience	Where and When	IMC Options
Need Arousal	Assume at least latent interest in cruising (category need) Stimulate awareness of our line (recall awareness) Tentative positive attitude toward cruising on our line for next major holiday (brand attitude)	Experienced cruiser Interested in cruising Travel agents	In home Travel agent's office	Broadcast advertising Direct mail to cruise customer Direct mail to travel agents
Information Search and Evaluation	Provide enough information to convince target (brand attitude) Gain positive intention (brand purchase intention)	Experienced cruiser Interested in cruising Travel agents	In home Travel agent's office	Print advertising P-o-p
Purchase	Act on positive intention (brand attitude and brand purchase intention)	Experienced cruiser Interested in cruising	Home (via telephone) Travel agent's office	Broadcast advertising Print promotions Direct mail to customers
Usage	Reinforce decision (brand attitude)	Cruisers	On ship	Loyalty promotion Premium promotion

As people look for information, our communication tasks change. Since taking a cruise vacation is a high involvement decision, we must now go further, providing enough information to convince the potential cruiser that now is the time to plan a cruise, and we are the best choice. The best way of accomplishing this is with print advertising where we can use longer copy, and point-of-purchase material for travel agents. This point-of-purchase or merchandising material could include posters and banners, as well as brochures. The next stage in the decision process is the actual purchase of the tickets. The specific communication task at this point is to get people to act upon the positive intentions they have formed. Ongoing broadcast advertising will keep the idea and our cruise line salient, and well-timed price promotions in newspapers or magazines could help trigger the decision. Additional direct mail promotion to previous cruisers would serve the same purpose.

Finally, during the cruise we will want to reinforce the decision. This is the point at which brand attitude should be at its highest, and it would make sense to reinforce this with specific promotions that might include on-board premiums or the initiation of a loyalty program.

With this completed IMC Task Grid we have laid out the strategy required to meet our communication objectives, along with the best marketing communication options to accomplish the job. As we have been pointing out all along, this type of planning is what IMC is really all about. Even if we end up only using advertising, or perhaps a direct mail promotion, we have engaged in IMC planning. We have looked at the communication problem confronting us, and considered the best IMC options to meet it.

Looking at our hypothesized IMC Task Grid for a cruise vacation, an IMC Media Budget Allocation Grid can easily be developed. Figure 7.10 illustrates what one might look like. Across the top we have filled in the Communication Tasks that were identified, and down the side are the various IMC options that were chosen to implement the campaign. Actually, specific media should be included here (e.g., cable TV, newspaper, brochures, etc.) but for our example we are using general types of media. In this example, advertising-oriented messages have been chosen as the primary means of communication, reinforced by various promotions. Because the communication tasks reflect what we need to do along the various stages of the decision process, it also serves as a timeline. The shaded areas indicate times when a particular option is not needed.

What the grid shows is that we would be using broadcast advertising ongoing to maintain awareness and reinforce a positive feeling (essential for a high involvement/transformational decision). Print advertising will be used to help provide the information a potential cruiser will want in order to arrive at a positive intention to cruise with us. Notice that we do not expect this to necessarily get people to actually act upon their positive intention. The plan is to utilize a promotion that will be running in newspapers and perhaps magazines to accomplish that communication task. Direct mail will be used to reach highly targeted prospects, delivering a general advertising message for the early stages of the decision process, as well as

Figure 7.10
Cruise Vacation IMC Media Budget Allocation Grid

IMC Communication Options	Communication Tasks				
	Create awareness and tentative interest	Provide information to convince	Seek positive intent	Action on interest	Reinforce decision
Primary: Broadcast advertising					■
Print advertising				■	■
Direct mail			■	■	■
Secondary: P-o-p					
Direct mail	■				
Print promotion	■				■

incentive promotions to stimulate actual purchase. Various point-of-purchase material will be prepared for use by travel agents, as well as on the cruise ships.

We now know what we need to do, and it only remains to allocate budgets to accomplish the tasks. One of the real advantages of this Budget Allocation Grid is that it permits you to see at a glance where, and importantly *why*, dollars are being spent. If adjustments must be made, for example because there is simply not enough money to satisfy the MEF requirements of the media selected, these adjustments can be seen within the context of the overall IMC program.

Chapter Notes

[1] D. E. Schultz, "Integration and the Media: Maybe Your Approach Is Wrong," *Marketing News*, June 21, 1993: 15.

[2] This point is discussed in an article headlined "Revisiting Ad Reach, Frequency" in *Advertising Age*, November 27, 1995.

[3] John Rossiter and Larry Percy first introduced this idea of minimum effective frequency in their book *Advertising and Promotion Management* (New York: McGraw-Hill, 1987).

[4] This is the basic formula presented by Rossiter and Percy in *Advertising and Promotion Management*.

[5] Rossiter and Percy, *Advertising Communications and Promotion Management*.

CHAPTER EIGHT

Identifying IMC Opportunities

Is IMC appropriate for all marketers? In one really important sense the answer is "yes." It is always appropriate to look at any communications question in terms of whether advertising or promotion tactics will best satisfy the communication objectives, and to look for the best means of delivering the message. But this does not mean that an integrated marketing communications program will always *be* the solution for all marketers in all situations. So far in this book we have dealt with how to strategically approach the implementation of an IMC program, and how to plan an IMC campaign. What we have *not* dealt with are the many complex issues involved in actually implementing IMC. For example:

- Is the marketer receptive to the idea?

- Does the marketer's decision-making structure make IMC planning possible?

- Are there incentives, or more likely, disincentives, to IMC in the current marketing structure (e.g., established relationships with suppliers of various advertising or promotion products)?

We will talk more about these potential problems in the next chapter. For the time being we shall continue to assume that there are no attitudinal or philosophical barriers to the strategic integration of a marketing communications program.

When IMC IS Likely to Be Needed

Perhaps the single best key to identifying a need for an IMC program is the complexity of the market with which we are dealing. The more complex, the more likely it will be that multiple or novel solutions will be required. Many things can contribute to the complexity of a communication problem. The most obvious is multiple communication objectives, but there are others that involve the target audience, the product or service itself, and the distribution of the product or service, as outlined in Figure 8.1.

Target Audience Complexity. There are a number of target audience considerations that lead to complexity in planning and delivering marketing communications. To begin with, the more people involved in the decision process, the more difficult the communication task. In the simple case, where one person plays all of the roles in the decision, such as someone looking for a snack in the afternoon for an energy boost, a straightforward message to a single individual is all that is needed. But as more people become involved in the decision, the potential need for multiple messages through a variety of media or delivery systems increases. This can happened everywhere from a family where children are lobbying parents for a special treat, to a large company planning to update its word processing systems in all of its departments.

Product or Service Complexity. If the product or service is highly technical or innovative, the communication task can be more complex. For example, when a new consumer electronics product is introduced, people need to be made aware of it, and interest stimulated. But they also will want a high level of information to complete what is usually a high involvement decision. If a number of models are available, again the information requirements will be greater. Even with seemingly less complex

---

Figure 8.1
Market Complexity

	Indications of Complexity
Target Audience	• Multiple people involved in the decision
	• Audiences with conflicting interests
	• Different media habits
Product or Service	• Highly technical or innovative
	• Variety of models
	• Multiple attributes
Distribution	• Highly influential in decision
	• Limited or specialized

---

products, if the brand represents multiple attributes and can satisfy diverse consumer needs, this opens up opportunities for IMC. For example, dehydrated soups can be marketed as soup or as a cooking ingredient; as great for lunch or good to take on a camping trip.

Distribution Complexity. An often-overlooked opportunity for IMC can be found in the distribution for a product or service. This goes beyond simple trade promotions. Many delivery systems have a great deal of influence on a brand being chosen. A good example would be travel agents, who almost always will have a significant influence on everything from minor considerations such as what hotel to stay at or what car to rent, to a major decision such as what cruise line to select for a Caribbean cruise.

Recognizing IMC Opportunities

If there is complexity in our market, as we have just seen, it is likely that some sort of IMC program will be needed. A simple advertising campaign or promotion is unlikely to be able to deal effectively with complex markets. But even in relatively simple or uncomplicated markets, there are usually opportunities for IMC.

You will remember from Chapter 3 that after a Behavioral Sequence Model has been developed for your product or service, in conjunction with the brand's target audience objective and communication strategy, you must decide whether or not an IMC program makes sense. The BSM provides a detailed and dynamic picture of the target market in terms of the overall decision process. Because of this, it is the perfect vehicle for identifying potential opportunities for utilizing various advertising and promotion messages. It is from the BSM that we construct the IMC Task Grid. In other words, it is the BSM that helps us recognize whether our communication task requires an IMC program, as outlined in Figure 8.2, and if so, helps us determine the best way of putting one together.

The BSM is an invaluable planning tool, helping us identify IMC opportunities. To underscore its usefulness in helping us recognize IMC opportunities, let us review again some of the things we discussed in Chapter 3.

A BSM utilizes a flow chart format to identify where a target audience is taking action or making decisions that will ultimately affect purchase. It identifies the major behavioral stages preceding, including, and following purchase or use. Then for each stage in the decision process it summarizes roles involved, where it occurs, when, and how. As you review all of this

---

Figure 8.2
BSM Implications That Would Suggest the Need for IMC

- The complexity of the target audience
- The complexity of distribution
- The complexity of the purchase decision
- Short- versus long-term communication objectives
- The need to isolate segments
- Need for multiple messages
- Opportunities for unique message delivery
- Opportunities for trade incentives
- Likely importance of retail messages

---

information, you are in a perfect position to organize your objectives and identify those points at which advertising and promotion may be most effectively employed.

We introduced two "generic" BSMs, suggesting that decisions important to eventual purchase or use are made at three or four major stages: need arousal, information search and evaluation (when the decision is high involvement), purchase, and usage. Remember, however, these labels are not all that important. What *is* important is that you begin to think about points in the consumer's decision process at which advertising or promotion can be influential.

As we saw, decision stages can be added, modified, or deleted to suit particular target audiences, product categories, or even brands. For example, someone loyal to a brand will be unlikely to engage in much information search and evaluation, even if the decision originally was high involvement. This would have an important influence on how this segment should be treated in terms of IMC planning. Brand loyals would not likely be interested in the message required to provide information to those less loyal.

While we can use the stages of the generic model as a starting point, the more you are able to tailor-make a behavioral sequence model for each marketing situation where marketing communication is needed, the more clearly it will suggest appropriate IMC applications.

Suppose we were the advertiser for a new product entry into a frequently purchased packaged goods product category: something like the new laundry detergent or fabric softener discussed in Chapter 3. How does the BSM help us recognize IMC opportunities here? If we feel that a single person is likely to play all of the roles involved (which would make sense for something like laundry detergent or fabric softener), then we know that we only have one role-player to worry about. However, we must still be concerned about whether that person only requires a single message to stimulate purchase, or whether several messages, perhaps delivered in different ways, would be necessary. Since we are talking about a new product, we will probably need more than one delivery system. For example, we know from Chapter 4 that broadcast advertising does a great job of raising people's awareness and awakening latent interest in a product. Unfortunately, most packaged goods categories do not excite the consumer, so it is quite easy for people to forget about the new product. For that reason, it would make sense to perhaps provide an incentive for trial with a coupon, and some sort of in-store display or shelf-talker to arrest the shopper's attention and remind him or her of the interest in the product that the advertising generated.

If all we did was advertise, there would be no guarantee that the shoppers would spot the item at the point of purchase because their behavior in the store is so routinized. In this example, broadcast advertising would be great for driving up need, but additional help may be needed when the actual purchase decision is made; help traditional advertising would not provide. This would be made clear from the BSM, as it reminds us that even though only one person is involved in the decision, the decision is not finalized all in a moment. Initial interest is aroused, but will likely lie latent until re-aroused in the store.

What if our new product is a children's snack? Here we could imagine at least two different people involved in the decision process: a child as initiator, influencer, and user; and a parent as influencer, decider, and purchaser. Again, as we saw in Chapter 3, the BSM might raise questions such as:

- Do we need different messages for child and parent to create awareness and interest in the snack, or simply different media for delivery?

- Is an incentive necessary for either the child or parent?

- Will an aid to recognition, such as a special display or shelf-talker, be necessary to remind the parent of the child's interest?

There are, of course, no "standard" answers to any of these questions. However, from the BSM you are alerted to the many possible marketing communications options that might be required. Beyond this, the BSM can also help you pinpoint:

- The complexity of the target audience

- The complexity of the distribution

- The complexity of the purchase decision
- Short- versus long-term communication objectives
- The need to isolate segments
- Need for multiple messages
- Opportunities for unique message delivery
- Opportunities for trade incentives
- Likely importance of retail messages

We have seen how complexity in the market in and of itself implies a need for IMC. The BSM will help alert you to more subtle complexities that are more a function of how consumers make decisions than of actual market conditions. For example, the roles played by various members of the target audience may add a complexity not otherwise easily noticed; and the ways in which information is gathered may signal *consumer-perceived* complexity within distribution that might otherwise be overlooked.

But the most important insight into the need for IMC and the guidance for strategic IMC planning provided by the BSM is related to message needs. As we look at how people go about making decisions in a category, the more complex the process, the greater the need for multiple options to deal with that complexity. If the decision is one that builds over time, such as the decision to buy a new car, the BSM will help identify short versus long-term communication objectives. Continuing with the automotive example, over the long term one must nurture an image for a vehicle that will help bring it into the consumers' considered set when they begin to think about a new car, but also provide detailed information and incentives for the short term when the final choice is being made. The need for an IMC program under these circumstances would be obvious from the BSM.

The roles people play, and the number of people involved in the decision, may suggest a need to isolate particular segments or a need for multiple messages. When, where, and how various stages of the decision process occur may suggest opportunities for unique message delivery. How important is the trade in affecting the decision? How much of the decision takes place in the store? Answers to such questions may suggest an opportunity for trade incentives or the likely importance of retail messages.

Because the BSM provides us with such a detailed overview of all the important aspects of how consumers make choices in a category, it is the ideal means for helping us identify IMC opportunities.

Using the BSM to Pinpoint IMC Opportunities

We have presented at some length now various ways in which insight may be drawn from a behavioral sequence model and used to access opportunities for IMC. In order to help pull all this together and demonstrate how one goes about actually using a BSM in this way, consider the hypothesized BSM shown in Figure 8.3 for a word processing system. Suppose you are marketing an innovative new word processing system, and have developed this BSM of how companies go about deciding upon introducing new systems into their operations.

Given this understanding of the decision process, what does it tell us about how best to effect the decision with marketing communication? Let us think through this process, which is in effect what you would be doing in developing an IMC Task Grid. It is obvious that this is a complex decision process, with multiple potential target audiences. As we look at the BSM, there is no doubt that an IMC program of some kind will be needed. Can we really imagine that a single advertising campaign, let alone a promotion of some kind, would be able to do the job? Of course not.

Looking at the need arousal stage we see that a number of people might be involved. At the simplest level, the users of the current system might be complaining to their manager that they can't get the increasing work load out on time. On the other hand, the manager in charge may be dissatisfied with the quality of the work, as the result of seeing or hearing about better alternatives. The users' or managers' need may be aroused without marketing communications if the work is falling behind, but if we wish to help stimulate need, some form of marketing communication will be required. Since we are marketing a *new* system, it will be necessary to communicate with both those involved as initiators within a company as well as those in the trade who will be asked to carry and "push" the new system. At the very least there will be two audiences participating in the need arousal stage who must be aware of your new system and begin to form a positive attitude toward it.

Once initial interest has been aroused, there will be an information search and evaluation stage as potential users and trade form attitudes about the positive and negative aspects of the various alternative systems available. The same individuals who were involved as initiators will probably fill the role of influencers as well. But others may also play a part. Consultants may be called in, and at some point during the evaluations senior management will become involved also. Do we want to use the same messages for everyone involved? While the messages to the trade (both consultants and distributors), users, and managers might be basically

Figure 8.3
BSM for a Word Processing System

Consideration at Each Stage	Decision Stage			
	Need Arousal	**Information Search and Evaluation**	**Purchase**	**Usage**
Decision roles involved	Users of current system and their managers as initiator Dealers or outside consultants as initiator	User/manager as influencer Dealers or outside consultants as influencers Senior management as decider	Manager and senior manager as decider and purchaser Purchasing agent as purchaser	User/manager as user
Where stage is likely to occur	In office	In office or house At dealer	In office or at dealer	In office
Timing of stage	Increase in work load or awareness from outside source	1–3 months following need arousal	After review of evaluation	After installation of system
How it is likely to occur	Can't keep up with work load Hear about new system from other sources (e.g., sales call)	Talking with dealers, consultants, or other users Review material or system	Look for best price or system and order	Using new system

the same, the medium of delivery will certainly vary. Messages to senior management will certainly be different. They are not interested in the technical material, but they are interested in "value" issues. There would appear to be a number of different marketing communication opportunities at this stage in the decision process. Additionally, if you do not already have a database in place, it would be a good time to begin one. If there is one, it should be updated during this stage.

At the purchase stage, managers and senior management will assume the role of decider, and a member of these groups, or perhaps a purchasing agent, will be involved in the actual purchase. What messages, if any, might we wish to deliver at this stage that differ from earlier material? The trade may wish to follow up with an incentive promotion; you may wish to send direct mail to those the trade has indicated have shown interest in your new system.

Finally, what do we want to do during the usage stage? At the very least, you will probably want to do something to reinforce the manager's choice of your new system. Some form of direct mail would make sense, but so too would general advertising that reinforces your overall brand image. This positioning affects not only the manager, but also those who are actually using the new system.

Many of those who are studying IMC today point out the importance of a solid understanding of the consumer in the effective application of IMC programs.[1] In fact, it is felt that you must look carefully at how consumers behave and see the world before you can develop an IMC program. We agree completely, and have offered the BSM as an ideal way of gaining this insight. It is indeed this insight into the consumer, more than anything else, that will help you identify opportunities for IMC.

Chapter Note

[1] Good discussion of the importance of the consumer in IMC may be found in the Don Schultz, Stanley Tannenbaum, and Robert Lauterburn book *Integrated Marketing Communications* (Lincolnwood, IL: NTC Business Books, 1993) and the chapter by Jeri Moore and Esther Thorson, "Strategic Planning for Integrated Marketing Communications Programs: An Approach to Moving from Chaotic toward Systematic," in E. Thorson and J. Moore (Eds.), *Integrated Communication* (Mahwah, NJ: Lawrence Erlbaum Associates, 1996), 135–152.

CHAPTER NINE

Problems in IMC Implementation

Before we look at some case histories of effective IMC campaigns in the final chapter, it would be useful to examine some of the barriers to implementing IMC. This book has dealt with the strategic thinking that underlies effective IMC programs, and has presented a number of aids to facilitate that kind of thinking and planning. After reading all of this you may well wonder "Why doesn't everyone do this?" Unfortunately, there are a number of potential roadblocks to the implementation of IMC. While it is beyond the scope of this book to offer solutions to these problems, because they are well outside the areas we have been addressing (the reader interested in some possible solutions is referred to Schultz et al.[1]), it is nonetheless a good idea to be aware of the sorts of problems you are likely to run into in trying to implement a successful IMC program.

The single biggest problem revolves around the decision-making structure of most marketing organizations. The structure or organizational make-up of a firm, and the way managers think about or approach marketing questions frequently pose problems in trying to implement IMC programs. While this is far and away the biggest potential roadblock, there are at least three other areas that can cause problems: managers' perceptions of IMC, compensation considerations, and current marketing trends. We shall discuss each of these four areas.

The Decision-Making Structure

In discussing several barriers to integration, Schultz[2] has identified something we see as a key to problems in implementing IMC. He points out that "integration requires communication across brands, SBUs, and functional specialties," yet "almost all organizations have spent their time developing vertical communication programs." The result is a need for *horizontal* relationships struggling within a *vertical* organization. This leads to problems at the organizational level, where parallel structures, multiple departments, and functional specialties discourage the kind of communication *between* specialties required for IMC planning. This type of problem is epitomized by the brand management concept, and recent moves by some large packaged goods companies to category or channel management is only likely to make the problem worse.

It should be clear from what we have presented in this book that IMC requires a central planning expertise in marketing communication. With diffused resources, individual manager relationships with marketing communication agencies and vendors, and (critically) a lack of incentive to cooperate, it is no wonder there are problems when it comes to effectively developing and implementing IMC programs.

There are two components to a firm's decision-making structure that contribute to these problems: organizational structure and what we might call organizational character, or the way an organization "thinks."

Organizational Structure

Although there is broad agreement among marketing managers (as discussed in Chapter 1) over the need for IMC, the very organizational structure of many marketing companies stands in the way of it being effectively implemented. As Schultz and his colleagues have put it, "There is little doubt that organizational structures are one of the largest barriers to IMC in most organizations."[3] At the core of this problem is an organization's ability to manage the interrelationships of information and materials among the various agencies and vendors involved in supplying marketing communication services. There are a number of specific structural factors that can make this difficult.

The Low Standing of Marketing Communication in an Organization. Unfortunately, for too many marketers, their marketing communication has a very low priority within the organization. For many in top management, spending money on marketing communication is a luxury that can be afforded only when all else is going well. One of the fastest ways for someone concerned with the financial statement to send large chunks of cash to the bottom line is to not spend budgeted marketing communication dollars.

With this sort of attitude, it is not surprising that those most responsible for marketing communication occupy lower-level positions within the organization. True, senior management does reserve the right to approve a campaign, and often does. But it would be rare indeed to find senior management involved in the *planning* of marketing communication. Rather, it is generally somewhat junior brand managers (or their equivalent) who do the actual strategic planning, and the results of their work are passed on up the management ladder for approval. Even at companies where there are specific managers for advertising or promotion, these managers will have little power within the organization, and almost never final responsibility for the budget. Final decision on the budget will be with those managers doing the actual marketing.

We have always found this very short-sighted. As one brand manager put it, can you think of any other part of a business where decisions involving millions of dollars are made with so little management involvement? If even half the average packaged goods brand ad budget were going into bricks and mortar, no doubt everyone including the board of directors would be involved!

Adding to this problem is the trend toward decentralized decision making pointed out by Schultz.[4] With more and more people empowered to make decisions at lower and lower levels, it makes it very difficult, if not impossible, to ensure an integrated marketing communication program.

Specialization. To effectively manage IMC, those in charge ideally will be marketing communication generalists. Yet where do you find such a person in today's marketing organizations? In fact, what one is most likely to find in companies are people specializing in a particular area; and these specialists rarely talk with each other. They have their own budgets, their own suppliers, and jealously guard the areas they control. The problem becomes even more complex when one considers the marketing communication suppliers these specialists use. Each being a specialist in a particular area (e.g., advertising, direct mail, merchandising), they naturally advocate their own solutions for marketing communication. By their very nature, whether intraorganizational or between suppliers, these specialists will want to keep communications programs separate.

Given the narrow focus and understanding of these specialists, it is very difficult to bring them together in the first place, let alone expect them to have the broad understanding of many marketing communication options necessary for effective IMC planning. But even if they did have this understanding, getting them to give up control, especially when it is unlikely to be financially advantageous (which we shall discuss more specifically later), is a lot to ask. Yet this is precisely what is necessary for IMC to work within an organization.

Organizational Character

In addition to the problems inherent in the way most marketing organizations are structured, there are more intangible aspects of an organization's thinking and behavior that also pose problems for implementing IMC. We have just seen how traditional organizational structure can impede the flow of information and ideas within the organization. Because of this type of structural barrier, it is very difficult for an entire company to share a common understanding of that company's marketing communication.

Yet it is important for everyone working at a company to understand and communicate the appropriate "image" in any marketing communication. Anyone who has any contact with customers must reflect the image projected by the company's marketing communications. This means store clerks, sales force, telephone operators, receptionists; all are a part of a company's marketing communication, and hence in many ways are IMC "media." Too often only those directly involved with the marketing communication program are familiar with it, and this can be a serious problem.

Financial Emphasis. Another important aspect of the character of an organization that bears upon IMC implementation is the misguided emphasis upon financial rather than consumer considerations in the development of marketing strategy. Schultz and his colleagues talk about some of the problems that come from this increasing reliance upon financial analysis to guide marketing strategy.[5] They point out that the attitude of most managers is to let financial considerations drive their thinking when setting marketing objectives, rather than consumer wants or needs. But as they suggest, and as we have demonstrated throughout this book, the consumer is at the center of IMC planning. IMC requires an understanding of how consumers make decisions and behave. When a marketer's attention is more financially focused than consumer focused, the planning environment will be less likely to successfully nurture IMC.

Culture of the Organization. How managers think is conditioned by both their own background and the culture of the company. This potential problem is then compounded in the IMC case when the culture of the marketer must interact with the culture of the marketing communication agencies and vendors. Managers from different companies are likely to have different views of what makes effective marketing communication. We will deal with this issue in more detail later when we look at the potential problems inherent in how different managers perceive IMC. Here we are simply considering their general views of things and how that will be tempered by organizational culture.

A great deal of literature on management addresses the idea that an organization will have its own defining culture, and that employees of the firm will absorb that culture. While that culture will not completely determine an individual manager's way of doing things, it will certainly have a significant impact upon its development.[6] This leads inevitably to such organizational feelings as "this is the way we do it"; "we've always done it this way"; "it works for us." We have all heard such comments when working with people from other companies or organizations (and have probably said things like this ourselves). Yet you can see how these kinds of attitudes can get in the way of integrated thinking and planning, both within an organization and working with outside agencies and vendors.

Manager Perceptions of IMC

How managers perceive IMC can often impede the implication of effective IMC as we have been discussing it in this book. When managers come from different backgrounds or different marketing communications specialties, either within the marketing organization or at marketing communication agencies or vendors, they are likely to have different perceptions of what constitutes integrated marketing communications and the roles various people should play in IMC planning and implementation.

Because of this, it is not surprising to find that there are any number of notions about how best to go about implementing integrated marketing communications. The 1991 study among marketing managers discussed in the first chapter found a variety of opinions about how IMC should be achieved.[7] Among the managers who said they were familiar with the term "integrated marketing communications" (a surprisingly low 59 percent), about 60 percent seem to look at the responsibility for IMC planning in roughly the same way as we do: Thirty-five percent felt they would collectively set communication strategies with all of the appropriate agencies and vendors, and then specific assignments would be executed by the best qualified agency or vendor. Another 25 percent felt they alone were responsible for setting the IMC strategy, but would then make specific assignments to appropriate agencies or vendors, and expect them to coordinate the execution.

We, of course, have argued that while the marketer must take the lead in IMC planning, strategy should be worked out among all relevant parties, who then execute creative work guided by the common creative brief(s), coordinated through the marketer. Among the remaining managers, 25 percent felt that they would work with one agency in setting strategy, and then leave it to that agency to execute everything (the notion of full-service agencies or "one-stop shopping" encouraged by some advertising agencies); and 7 percent felt they would set the communication strategy and then have it executed by the individual agency or vendor most appropriate for each task (advertising, direct mail, merchandising, etc.).

Resistance to Change

Different perceptions of IMC will certainly mediate effective implementation. But much more troubling is the natural resistance to change that the idea of IMC is likely to trigger, making it difficult to implement despite general acceptance of the benefits. Two Northwestern University professors have identified several concerns that are likely to cause employee resistance to integrated planning.[8] We have already discussed generally the problems that can come from trying to mix specialists in different areas of marketing communication. This is really at the heart of what they see as the key concern likely to lead to employee resistance to IMC.

The most serious concern is probably a fear that the manager responsible for IMC planning will not fully appreciate someone else's area of expertise. This is a problem that is especially compounded when advertising takes the lead (which it should in most cases, as we have seen) because of long-held feelings that advertising managers simply do not understand or even consider other means of marketing communications (which unfortunately, is too often the case). This is aggravated by the short-term tactical experience, for example, of those working in promotion versus the more long-term thinking of advertising managers. If employees feel the IMC manager does not fully appreciate their worth, they are certain to worry about where their specialties will fit in department budgeting, and fear their jobs will become less important or even redundant. Such feelings could easily cause resistance to the implementation of IMC planning.

Politics and Power

Another way of looking at some of these issues of resistance to change is in terms of both intraorganizational and interorganizational politics. It doesn't matter if the motivation is individual self-interest or an actual belief in the superiority of one's way of doing things, the result is the same.[9] People, departments, and organizations want power and the rewards that go with it. Too often managers and their staff believe they will be giving up too much if they implement effective integrated marketing communications planning. Compensation (which we take up next) is only one aspect of this problem. There are feelings of prestige and position, that have in many cases been hard-won, that the combining of responsibilities required by IMC seem to threaten. This can be a very difficult problem.

Compensation

Compensation issues are less of a direct problem within a marketing organization than with agencies and vendors. Still, even there it is a problem. We have already referred to several circumstances where marketing communication specialists within a company are likely to be concerned about the importance of their position in a realigned IMC-oriented marketing communication group. Such concerns lead quite naturally to worries about salaries and promotion, and dampen enthusiasm for IMC.

But the real concern over compensation lies with those agencies and vendors that serve the marketing communication needs of the marketer. This has certainly proved to be a stumbling block to many large advertising agencies that have tried to offer their clients a full range of marketing communication services. Group managers at these agencies are traditionally rewarded based upon their total billings and income. That being the case, how likely is it that the management of the advertising group will suggest to their client that perhaps they would be better off spending more of their money on direct marketing, even if there is a direct marketing group at the agency, let alone if the work would need to be done elsewhere?

Somehow these managers (at least within an agency or vendor offering multiple communication services) must be compensated without regard to how much is spent on their particular specialty, but in terms of the overall business. Without such a scheme, effective IMC is impossible because those in charge of a particular type of marketing communication will be more concerned with "selling" their specialty, not with how their specialty will best contribute to an overall IMC program.

This problem is aggravated when a number of competing agencies or vendors are asked to work together. In fact, this is the primary reason many agencies and vendors have sought to provide a number of different types of marketing communications in order to maximize their chances of retaining business. Such firms have either tried to create groups within their organization to provide a variety of marketing communication services or have merged with other suppliers. While such moves offer the potential for higher profit or greater financial stability overall for the agency or vendor, as we discussed above, it is not easy to manage the compensation between the competing specialties.

It should not be surprising that any company will want to maintain its profitability in a changing world. In doing this, it should likewise not be surprising that they will be more interested in their own financial well-being than in providing the best overall IMC program for their clients. This underscores the need for tight control of planning by the marketer.

Trends in Marketing

A number of trends in marketing also pose problems for effectively implementing IMC. Perhaps the most confounding is the trend toward IMC! As Schultz has pointed out, when the subject of integration comes up, the most likely response is "We already do that."[10] Of course they probably do not, at least in the way in which we have been considering IMC. The problem is that in some limited ways they may, or at least feel that they do. This makes it difficult to get managers thinking in different ways, or to acknowledge that they still have a way to go before they are effectively planning for IMC.

One of the reasons many marketing organizations feel they are already practicing IMC is the trend running from the 1980s of marketers more and more doing their own communications strategic planning, relying less upon their agencies and vendors. The "partnership" that characterized earlier relationships has all but disappeared, driven away by many factors. With the focus of communication strategy within the marketing organization, its communication suppliers are less inclined to maintain planning resources, or to even think much about planning and strategy beyond the specific assignments they are given. Now with even more financial pressure upon marketers, there are cutbacks in the in-house resources necessary for effective strategic planning. What we too often have are marketers with an overload of information, but without sufficient staff for analysis. Their agencies and vendors no longer have the information, or expertise in many cases. Effective IMC requires a cooperative effort between the marketer and communication suppliers, yet between them sufficient resources may simply not exist.

Niche Marketing and Micromarketing

A major trend in marketing has been niche marketing and micromarketing, increasingly popular ways of addressing complex or diverse markets. Unfortunately, too often marketers believe each segment requires individual and distinct communication programs. After all, if different markets are looking for different things, doesn't this mean each segment requires a different communication program? No. If a single *brand* is involved, one IMC program is still likely to be most effective. The executions need not be identical, but the overall look and feel must be if one is to maximize the impact of communication dollars. We discussed this in much detail in Chapter 4. Even if under some circumstances it is better to position a brand differently to different segments, within each sub-market you should still be approaching the strategic development of the communications within the framework of IMC planning.

As bad as multiple positions or images for a brand are, it is just as bad to *change* images frequently. Images and messages should evolve, not change radically. This can be a real danger with micromarketing, and also with the flexibility of direct marketing. These techniques offer important targeting ability, but messages that are continuously changing are confusing for consumers. It is important to carefully guard against the temptation to ignore the disciplines associated with IMC because you are focusing narrowly on a particular group or market segment.

Overcoming the Barriers

Although the need for integrated marketing communications is widely understood and accepted, as the foregoing discussion makes clear, the path to implementation is hampered by many potential barriers. We have summarized these potential barriers in Figure 9.1. Yet these barriers are not insurmountable, and the rewards from effective IMC make the effort worthwhile. By becoming aware of these potential problems, and identifying them within your own organization, you are on the way toward overcoming them.

Figure 9.1
Potential Barriers to Implementing IMC

Decision-Making Structure	Vertical organizational structures when cooperation is needed between functions
	Low standing of marketing communication function within many marketing organizations
	Too many specialists working independently
	Limited understanding of the marketing communication message within the organization
	Financial considerations placed ahead of consumer considerations
	Rigid organizational culture
Perception of IMC	No common understanding of what constitutes IMC
	Other marketing communication specialties do not understand
	Fear over who will be in charge
Compensation	Without budget control, specialists fear they will lose position
	Individual rewards are linked to use of specialists' specific type of marketing communication, not to the overall program
Trends in Marketing	Feeling that the organization already uses IMC
	Lack of staff resources in organization and at agencies and vendors
	Belief that niche marketing and micro-marketing don't need IMC

We do not pretend that dealing with these problem will be easy. After all, they go to the heart of how companies function day-to-day. The way decisions are made, the way an organization is structured, are all a part of the operational lifeblood of a company. Change requires trust, and this trust comes from a total understanding of what is involved, and the long-term potential.

The aim of this book is to provide the understanding required to appreciate and implement effective IMC. The final chapter presents three case studies showing how the principles and techniques we have introduced have been applied, leading to effective communication that enabled marketers to not only reach, but to surpass their marketing goals.

Chapter Notes

[1] Schultz, Tannenbaum, and Lauterborn, *Integrated Marketing Communications* (see Chap. 1, n. 1).

[2] D. E. Schultz, "How to Overcome the Barriers to Integration," *Marketing News,* July 19, 1993: 16.

[3] Schultz, Tannenbaum, and Lauterborn, *Integrated Marketing Communications.*

[4] D. E. Schultz, "How to Overcome the Barriers to Integration."

[5] Schultz, Tannenbaum, and Lauterborn, *Integrated Marketing Communications.*

[6] D. Prensky, J. A. McCarty, and J. Lucas, "Integrated Marketing Communication: An Organizational Perspective," in E. Thorson and J. Moore (Eds.), *Integrated Communication* (Mahwah, NJ: Lawrence Erlbaum Associates, 1996), 167–184.

[7] T. R. Duncan and S. E. Everett, "Client Perceptions of Integrated Marketing Communications," *Journal of Advertising Research,* May/June 1993: 30–39.

[8] L. A. Petrison and P. Wang, "Integrated Marketing Communication, Examining Planning and Executional Considerations," in E. Thorson and J. Moore (Eds.), *Integrated Communication* (Mahwah, NJ: Lawrence Erlbaum Associates, 1996), 153–165.

[9] This point is also made by Prensky, McCarty, and Lucas in "Integrated Marketing Communication: An Organizational Perspective."

[10] Schultz, "How to Overcome the Barriers to Integration."

CHAPTER TEN

IMC Applications: Three Case Studies

In this final chapter we shall take a look at how three marketers have implemented IMC programs, utilizing the strategic planning tools and thinking we have presented in this book. Each case is different, and represents a range of marketing communication problems. These cases have been chosen not only because they are excellent examples of how to successfully implement an IMC program, but also because they represent mid-size marketers. It is not just giants like IBM or Sara Lee (to name two companies that are heavily involved with IMC) that are or should be implementing IMC programs. *All* marketers should approach their marketing communication from an IMC perspective. They may not always need to utilize multiple means of communicating, but as we have seen, that is not what IMC planning is all about. IMC is a strategic planning discipline that will help you determine the best way to meet your communication objectives.

The first case offers an interesting communication problem. Lichtwer Pharma markets three different brand-name natural health supplements, with others likely to be added in the future. Their task is to market these different brands under the same general umbrella, gaining symmetry and efficiency, rather than as individual brands. In the second case, PAGETIME is rolling out a paging service into markets with widely differing category penetration, something that significantly affects message content. The third case involves a complicated decision process. Transitions Optical markets photosensitive lenses, where the consumers' decision to buy also includes their eye care professionals.

In each of these cases, by following the strategic direction outlined in this book, an effective IMC program was developed and implemented.

Lichtwer Pharma U.S.

Lichtwer Pharma introduced Kwai, an odor-free garlic tablet, to the United States in 1990. Since then two additional herbal remedies have joined Kwai: Ginsai Standardized Ginseng Extract and Ginkai Standardized Ginkgo Tablets. The challenge to Lichtwer Pharma was to bundle these three brand names and market them effectively with a single marketing communication program. The challenge clearly called for an IMC solution, and the results of their thinking are summarized in this section.

Marketing Background Worksheet Questions

Lichtwer Pharma markets three herbal supplements in a highly competitive market. While there is a strong potential within a large natural health supplement market, there are many alternatives available that compete for many of the same benefits; both alternative brands of garlic tablets, ginseng extract, and ginkgo tablets as well as alternative natural remedies. For Lichtwer Pharma to succeed, they must attract business from existing competition as well as attract current health supplement users who are not currently using these particular products. To accomplish this, marketing communications must tie the brands together in order to build upon the equity already established with Kwai, and provide a believable difference for products generally perceived to be commodities.

Key Target Audience Worksheet Questions

Sales are expected to come from both existing Kwai users as well as non-customers in the health supplement market. The trade plays an important role in the target audience because both pharmacists and health food store staff are known to be sources of information for health supplement users. Overall, the target audience is concerned about their health, and interested in health supplements. These people tend to be older, and are attracted to various remedies and supplements believed to help specific health or nutrition needs. For Kwai, this means adults with cholesterol concerns; for Ginsai those looking for more "energy"; and for Ginkai, those seeking to improve mental capacity.

Decision Roles. It is not uncommon for an individual adult to play all five roles in the decision to try and use herbal supplements. However, other adult family members or friends often play roles as initiators and influencers, talking about new products or brands, or new information they have learned about particular remedies or supplements. Outside of this rather personal circle, only health food store employees or pharmacists are likely to be involved in the decision process, playing an influencer role.

Key Communication Strategy Worksheet Questions

Since our target audience is made up of those already interested in health supplements, category need is assured. This means that our primary communication objectives will be the two universal objectives, brand awareness and brand attitude. Given the nature of these products, the brand awareness objective will be recognition. Marketing communications will always need to provide a good visual image of the package in order to promote easy recognition at the point of purchase. The brand attitude strategy is rather interesting. On the surface, trying different health supplements might be seen as low involvement, especially among this target audience (who are already category users, or at least favorably disposed). This may well be the case, but there are many alternative products competing for the same "remedy," and often different brands of the same product. Add to this the fact that it is often not easy to measure the results of using these products, especially in the short-term, and it would seem more likely that people will need to be convinced of their choice, overcoming the perceived risk attached in possibly wasting their effort and money on a supplement that does not perform. As a result, the safer assumption is that this will be a high involvement decision. The motivation, on the other hand, is clearly negative (problem avoidance, problem solution, or incomplete satisfaction), calling for an informational strategy. The brand attitude strategy is therefore high involvement/informational.

What we want people to do as a result of our marketing communication effort is become aware of the brands and be convinced of their efficacy and superiority over competitive alternatives, leading to trial and continued usage (our secondary communication objective).

BSM for Health Supplements

Having worked our way through the various worksheet questions we now are in a position to develop a Behavioral Sequence Model of the consumer decision process leading to the selection and use of health supplements. Since the decision is high involvement we know that an information search and evaluation stage will be required. In fact, the generic BSM for high involvement decisions fits the health supplement decision process perfectly. Need for a particular health supplement must be aroused, the potential user will then "check it out," and if they are convinced of its potential, will purchase the product and use it. Figure 10.1 shows how the high involvement generic BSM was used to model the decision process for health supplements.

The decision roles considered when we addressed the questions in the Target Audience Worksheet are allocated for each of the four decision stages. Need arousal is most likely to come from individual adults, family members, or friends after they have become aware of the product or brand through an article in a newspaper or magazine, advertising, or word-of-mouth. Piqued by this initial interest, they will enter an information search and evaluation stage, gathering information from various sources, where friends, family, or some other adult plays the role of influencer. During this stage pharmacists can play a significant role as an influencer, as might employees at health food stores. Once this information has been evaluated, the potential individual adult user will form an intention to try, playing a role as decider. This same individual adult or other family member will be the purchaser at the purchase stage of the decision process, ordering through the mail or by phone, or by visiting a pharmacy or health food store. Finally, the individual adult and/or family members will assume the role of user in the usage stage.

IMC Task Grid for Health Supplements

The development of the BSM provides an overview of how people are likely to go about making a decision to purchase and use a health supplement, and the people and factors that will be involved in that decision. As we have learned, the discipline involved in thinking through a BSM provides the first real step toward IMC strategy. By studying the BSM one is able to "see" where marketing communications might be effectively used. As we look at the BSM, it is clear that a single message using one primary type of marketing communication will not be sufficient to effectively market the Lichtwer Pharma brands. This means it is necessary to complete an IMC Task Grid. Figure 10.2 lays out the IMC Task Grid that resulted from The St. George Group's (Lichtwer Pharma's agency) analysis of the health supplement BSM.

You will remember that the IMC Task Grid asks you to look at each stage in the consumer's likely decision process and develop appropriate communication tasks that address each communication objective, relate

Figure 10.1
BSM for Health Supplements

Consideration at Each Stage	Decision Stage			
	Need Arousal	**Information Search and Evaluation**	**Purchase**	**Usage**
Decision roles involved	Individual adults, family members, friends as initiators	Individual adult, family members, friends as influencer Individual adult as decider Pharmacist as influencer	Individual adult or family members as purchaser	Individual adult or family member as users
Where stage is likely to occur	In-home Word-of-mouth	In-home Pharmacy Health food stores Library	In-home response to promotion Health food store Pharmacy	In-home
Timing of stage	Upon awareness	Weeks immediately following initial awareness and interest	After convinced of benefit	Daily
How it is likely to occur	See or hear about product category or brand	Seek information from others, look up information, visit pharmacy or health food store	Phone or write-in order Visit pharmacy or health food store Visit HBA section of retail store	Taking supplement on daily basis

them to the appropriate segments of the target audience and their behavior, and then list appropriate advertising or promotion options that might effectively accomplish the tasks.

Figure 10.2

IMC Task Grid for Lichtwer Pharma Health Supplements

Decison Stage	Communication Task	Target Audience	Where and When	IMC Options
Need Arousal	Assume at least latent interest in herbal supplements (category need) Stimulate awareness of products and brands (recognition awareness) Tentative positive attitude for our brands (brand attitude)	Older adults Trade Middle-aged adults for selected products	In home Appropriate retail outlets	Television and print advertising for consumer Trade advertising
Information Search and Evaluation	Provide enough information to convince target (brand attitude) Gain positive intention to try brand (brand purchase intention)	Older adults Trade Middle-aged adults for selected products	In home Appropriate retail outlets	Radio and print advertising Print promotion P-o-p
Purchase	Act on positive brand intention (brand attitude and brand purchase intention)	Older adults Middle-aged adults for selected products	In home Appropriate retail outlets	Advertising Print promotion P-o-p
Usage	Reinforce decision (brand attitude) and brand usage (brand purchase intention)	Older adults Middle-aged adults for selected products	In home	Advertising Selective promotion

The communication tasks associated with need arousal reflect the brand awareness and brand attitude communication objectives. Because the target audience members are health supplement users, or at least have some interest in them, category need (as already noted) is assumed. This means we must first stimulate *recognition* brand awareness, providing a strong visual package association with the brand name for each of the three products. Additionally, some tentative interest in the specific product category and brand must be created. Television advertising is the best and fastest way to satisfy these objectives, while print advertising will help reinforce them both. At the same time, trade advertising will be required to help raise the salience of the product with the trade and set the stage for answering consumer inquiries in the next stage.

At the information search and evaluation stage the task is to provide enough information to convince the target audience that these products are worth trying, seeding a positive brand attitude, and to occasion an intention to try the *brand* (*not* any garlic or ginkgo tablet, or ginseng extract). This is the stage where marketing communications must fully effect the brand attitude and brand purchase intention communication objectives. We will need to reach the same target audience as in the need arousal stage. At this stage radio ads could help maintain brand salience, while print advertising and possible merchandising at the point-of-purchase can provide the detail necessary to help convince potential users of the brand's effectiveness.

The purchase stage for health supplements may occur at home via mail or phone order, or at appropriate retail outlets. Since Lichtwer Pharma products are only available at retail, advertising plays a critical role in retaining their brands' salience when confronted with direct marketing efforts of competitors. At the same time, coupon promotions also undercut direct marketing efforts and help remind potential users to buy. Point-of-purchase displays and other merchandising at retail will also serve to trigger brand recognition and remind the potential user of his or her intention to try the brand.

With usage, continued advertising and selective promotion reinforce the user's brand decision. Because short-term effects may be difficult to detect, it is important that users are continually reminded of their conviction that the Lichtwer Pharma brands offer an advantage over competitive alternatives.

The Lichtwer Pharma IMC Program

The IMC Task Grid in Figure 10.2 summarizes the strategic thinking for Kwai, Ginsai, and Ginkai marketing communication. We know from our discussions in Chapter 4 that a Primary Communication Creative Brief will be required to lay out the creative guidelines for the primary thrust of the IMC program. It is clear from what we know that a message-oriented campaign will be required, with the addition of some promotion in support. Awareness of category need and the Lichtwer Pharma's brands is essential, and this means primarily advertising.

Figure 10.3

Primary Creative Brief for Lichtwer Pharma Health Supplements

PRODUCT Kwai/Ginsai/Ginkai	JOB	DATE

KEY MARKET OBSERVATIONS
Competition not only with other brands of same products, but from other health supplements with perceived similar benefits

SOURCE OF BUSINESS
Current users of health supplements

CONSUMER BARRIER/INSIGHT
A large and often confusing health supplement market with little perceived product differentiation among "natural" supplements

TARGET MARKET
Generally older adults with positive interest/belief in benefits of health supplements

COMMUNICATION OBJECTIVES AND TASKS
Brand awareness recognition to raise brand salience and seed primary brand attitude "proven" positioning

BRAND ATTITUDE STRATEGY
High involvement/informational brand attitude strategy driven by motivation of problem-solution, problem avoidance, or incomplete satisfaction

BENEFIT CLAIM AND SUPPORT
Lichtwer Pharma brands are "proven." Support: independent testing documents performance claims

DESIRED CONSUMER RESPONSE
Belief that Lichtwer Pharma brands are superior to alternatives because they are "proven"

CREATIVE GUIDELINES
Tie "proven" to each brand's performance claims, providing campaign umbrella, and ensure consistent look and feel across brand executions

REQUIREMENTS/MANDATORY CONTENT
Refer to Kwai equity in Ginsai/Ginkai executions

The Primary Creative Brief for the Lichtwer Pharma IMC program is shown in Figure 10.3. The overall task confronting them was to break through the competitive clutter of competing products and brands in the health supplement market that includes garlic tablets, ginkgo tablets, and ginseng extracts. A key barrier to overcome is a perception that all of these products are pretty much the same: "natural" remedies. Because the company had invested millions of dollars in independent double-blind placebo-controlled tests with humans, it was felt that this would provide a believable and unique "proven" positioning for the brands.

Individual messages were developed for each of the three brands, but all under the "proven" umbrella. This primary benefit claim ties the brands together, while the individual messages address the particular health benefit of the specific brand. Additionally, a consistent look and feel to the executions provides further synergy among the brands, even though we are dealing with three different brand names. This consistency is desirable for all of the reasons discussed in Chapter 4, but it also encourages carry-over from the equity established with the earlier introduction of Kwai. Figure 10.4 illustrates the excellent execution of this consistent look and feel for the three brands.

You will also notice in these ads that the package too reflects a consistent look and feel. This is an often neglected aspect of IMC. We briefly mentioned this in Chapter 5. Your package is one of your most important vehicles for communicating your message. Understanding this, Lichtwer Pharma's agency developed a new package that included the "proven" seal and the primary brand attribute claim as part of the shelf-hanger attached to each package (see Figure 10.5). Here a creative idea developed for advertising, the "proven" seal, provided an opportunity to extend the message to p-o-p and into the home with new packaging. This is yet another example of the power implicit in effective IMC planning.

In addition to the consumer print advertising, both television and radio spots were created, consistent with the need to effectively deal with the ongoing decision process; advertising plays a role at each stage. To facilitate a positive brand purchase intention, a coupon promotion was developed. The FSI, as we saw in the Ginkai example discussed back in Chapter 2 (Figure 2.4), directly ties the consumer print ad to both the insert and the coupon itself. This congruence was also carried through in point-of-purchase merchandising, as well as with trade advertising, as you can see with the Kwai trade ad shown in Figure 10.6

Finally, we should note that while public relations is beyond the scope of this book, when one is able to utilize PR, it too should be consistent with the overall IMC program. In this case the agency also employed PR

Figure 10.4

Three Ads for Lichtwer Pharma Brands with a Consistent Look and Feel

to help further communicate the results of independent clinical testing of plant-based medicines, providing increased support and credibility for the IMC "proven" campaign.

Figure 10.5
A Package That Reflects the Lichtwer IMC Message

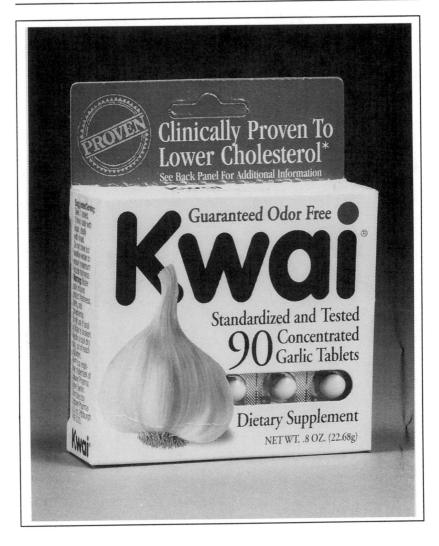

Figure 10.6

A Kwai Trade Ad Congruent with the Total IMC Program

IMC Media Budget Allocation Grid

You should now have a good sense of the IMC program that was developed for Lichtwer Pharma, and how it utilizes the strengths of various marketing communications options to address the communication tasks confronting the brands. A look at the IMC Media Allocation Grid shows just how it was implemented (Figure 10.7).

Broadcast advertising is used continuously to maintain brand salience and interest in the products. We know that television is the best way to address awareness, but not as effective on its own in providing the detail usually needed to convince consumers of a high involvement decision. This is why print advertising in magazines and coupon promotions are also included, to provide an opportunity for learning and stimulate interest in trying. But, at the same time, the television advertising continues to tie the brand names to the primary "proven" benefit claim in the consumer's mind.

This is also how radio is being used. We know from Chapter 7 that radio is not a good medium for recognition awareness or high involvement/informational brand attitude strategies. In this case, however, it is being used as an efficient secondary source for reinforcing the association of the brand names with the category need, and the primary "proven" benefit claim. Here again we see how IMC planning is able to integrate various media options to effect an overall objective when on its own a particular medium may be inappropriate.

Finally, the point-of-purchase merchandising provides an enhanced opportunity to recognize the brands and for consumers to remember their intentions to try or repeat purchase when at the store. Point-of-purchase requires prior exposure to the brand to work effectively, and that is accommodated by this plan.

Overall, media have been selected well, reinforcing each other and scheduled to maximize their strengths against the appropriate communication task. The IMC Media Budget Allocation Grid provides a good overview of how the IMC program was being implemented.

PAGETIME

This second case study presents a much different problem from the first. To begin with, PAGETIME is a service, and as the name implies, a paging service. It is also subject to significant regional variations in market conditions. This presents a real marketing communication challenge, one that requires careful strategic planning as the service is rolled out. On the surface, it may seem rather straightforward, perhaps not even requiring multiple communication options. But as we shall see as we learn more about the case, if marketing PAGETIME had not been approached through the discipline of IMC planning, there is little likelihood they would have been as successful as they have been. The IMC planning ensured that the right combination of marketing communication was used, and in the right way. Competitors use basically the same media, but not in an integrated way.

Figure 10.7					
IMC Media Budget Allocation Grid for Lichtwer Pharma					
IMC Communication Options	**Communication Tasks**				
	Create Awareness and Tentative Interest	Provide Information to Convince	Seek Positive Intent	Action on Intent	Reinforce Decision
Primary: television advertising					
magazine advertising	■				
Secondary: radio advertising					
coupon promotion	■	■			■
trade advertising			■	■	■
p-o-p	■	■	■		

IMC planning was also important in dealing with the unique partnership agreement PAGETIME has with Adelphia Cable. Adelphia Cable, a cable television provider, offers unique and highly targeted delivery channels for PAGETIME's marketing communication through their cable customer base. In effect, Adelphia Cable is the marketing arm of PAGETIME.

Marketing Background Worksheet Questions

PAGETIME is marketing a paging service through the Adelphia Cable customer base. As a service, it is billed on a monthly basis. However, one must obviously have a pager to subscribe to the service. PAGETIME will sell customers a quality Motorola pager or will activate any currently owned customer pager to the PAGETIME frequency, but they are not in the business of retailing pagers.

Assessing the market for PAGETIME is difficult. In 1995 they began rolling out the service in several East Coast markets. In some markets pager penetration in certain areas was as high as 98 percent, while in others as low as 11 percent. Clearly such differences needed to be taken into account when setting communication strategy. There are large competitors with telecommunications services such as AT&T and SkyTel offering paging services along with their cellular phone or two-way communications services, and there are smaller competitors such as American Paging and PageMart. The competitive positioning in each market also varies. Markets with heavy competition rely upon low monthly service fees, but require long-term commitments (e.g., one-year lease agreements or prepayment of a year's fees). In markets with little competition, monthly service fees are typically much higher. All markets are very price competitive. Most competitive paging services position their service for business-related activities such as sales, deliveries, and the need to stay in constant touch with clients or the home office. Source of business also varies by market. Clearly in markets with extremely high pager penetration business will come from existing paging service companies. In other markets, business will come from growing the category. Complicating this, within markets there are areas of high and low pager penetration.

The overall marketing objective was to capture significant share in high pager penetration markets, while expanding category need in those markets with low penetration. Continued usage would provide a recurring monthly income revenue stream. Marketing communications are expected to contribute to achieving these objectives by defining category need and firmly linking PAGETIME with this need.

Key Target Audience Worksheet Questions

Because PAGETIME is a new paging service, all usage will come from new customers to PAGETIME. However, depending upon the market, these may or may not be new paging service users. Also, because of their marketing relationship with Adelphia Cable, while all customers will be new to PAGETIME, it is expected that nearly all will be existing customers of Adelphia Cable. In terms of trial versus repeat usage, again because the service is new, we are looking at trial, even though many potential customer currently use a paging service. This complicates the target audience definition, because we must include both non-category users as well as existing users, depending upon the market. Unlike most products or services, there really is no trade involvement in the traditional sense. Because of PAGETIME's relationship with Adelphia Cable, there is no need to seek distribution. Adelphia Cable is the marketing channel, with direct broadcast cable lines into target market homes as well as direct mail access via monthly cable bills.

The consumer target audience is comprised of individuals and families, all under the age of 55. Research has suggested that older adults are simply not interested in the service. These people all have an interest in keeping in touch. The actual decision makers will be individual adults or household heads, although other family members and friends may certainly play roles in the decision.

Decision Roles. Looking closely at who is likely to be involved in the decision to subscribe to a paging service, one finds it a largely personal process. Even though it is a high involvement decision (as we will discuss later), there are not likely to be experts or specialists involved in the decision because it is unlikely to be a decision made at retail. If a single individual does not play all of the roles in the decision, the initiators and influencers are most likely to be among family or friends. In some cases, if the potential customer does shop for a pager, sales staff may play a role as an influencer. By and large, however, initiators and influencers will be personal acquaintances. The role of decider and purchaser will almost always be an individual adult, while the user may be a single person or multiple family members.

Key Communication Strategy Worksheet Questions

As our target audience consideration implies, we are dealing with two distinct target audience groups, with different communication needs. For those without pagers, category need is a required communication objective; but it is obviously assumed for those now using a paging service. The universal brand awareness and brand attitude communication objectives are both important. Brand awareness here will be recall: we want people to think of PAGETIME when the need for a paging service is aroused. The decision to either subscribe to a paging service or to switch services will be high involvement. The motivation for both target groups is negative, and most likely either problem avoidance or incomplete satisfaction. This means that the brand attitude strategy is high involvement/informational. With category need linked to our brand, and positive attitudes built toward the brand, it will also be necessary to generate brand purchase intention.

What we want people without pagers to do as a result of our marketing communication is become aware of the need for a paging service, become convinced that PAGETIME is the best service, and look into subscribing. For those already using a paging service, we want them to become aware of PAGETIME, be convinced it is a better alternative, and look into subscribing. Overall, the communication objective for the two target groups is the same, except that non-users of paging services must be convinced of the need as well as the brand. What this means is that a single communication strategy can be used, because the message content required to stimulate category need and its link to the brand among non-users will reinforce the link for potential switchers.

BSM for Paging Services

Having answered the key marketing background, target audience and communication strategy questions, we are able to work through a Behavioral Sequence Model of how consumers are likely to go about making a decision to try or change paging service. While we are dealing with two target groups, the overall decision process is actually the same for both groups. The only difference is how information will be used at various stages. Since the purchase decision is high involvement, some information search and evaluation must occur in order to convince potential customers of their decision. This means we can either use the generic high involvement BSM or some variation of it that more closely reflects the specific decision process for subscribing to a paging service. In this case, the Birmingham Group (PAGETIME's agency) developed a more specific model with four stages: need arousal, check-out paging services, subscribe to service, and usage and reinforcement (see Figure 10.8).

Figure 10.8
BSM for a Paging Service

Consideration at Each Stage	Decision Stage			
	Need Arousal	Check-out Paging Services	Subscribe to Service	Usage and Reinforcement
Decision roles involved	Individual adults, family, friends as initiator, influencer	Individual adults, family, friends as influencer Adult as decider Retail staff as influencer	Adult as decider and purchaser	Single or multiple family member as user
Where stage is likely to occur	In home Talking with friends	In home Talking with friends Retail outlet	In home	Ongoing
Timing of stage	Any time	From immediately after need arousal up to a few weeks later	After evaluation	Any time after sign-up
How it is likely to occur	Experience problem staying in touch Hear about	Seek information from friends See/hear advertising Inquire from paging services	Phone-in order	Any time need occurs or are reminded of need

At the need arousal stage, non-users of paging services must be made aware of how a paging service can help satisfy their need to "stay in touch," while potential switchers must be made aware of the new alternative. For both groups, initial interest must be aroused. This need arousal can be initiated and influenced by others, particularly friends and family, and for the non-users is most likely to occur when the potential customer is experiencing or has recently experienced a situation where a pager would have been helpful. Once interest is aroused, the target groups will begin the check-out paging services stage. This could begin as early as the initial need arousal. Again friends or family could be involved as influencers, or perhaps the staff at a retail location. This could occur either actively (e.g., calling someone) or passively (e.g., seeing advertising). It may or may not involve comparisons with other services for the current non-user (it obviously does for current users), but some consideration will be given to the decision because of the high involvement nature. If convinced to try or switch, potential customers will then make a final decision and contact the paging service to subscribe to the service. As they use the service, during usage and reinforcement, because it is a service, users will continuously evaluate both performance and need.

We should note here that the BSM with which we are concerned is for a paging *service*. Obviously, one must have a pager to use a paging service. This is why most paging services facilitate the acquisition of a pager. In the BSM this is accounted for during the check-out paging services stage. Here is where non-users of paging services will learn about pager options. While pagers are often an integral part of paging service marketing, it is important to realize that the decision to subscribe to a paging service is independent of a decision to acquire a specific pager.

IMC Task Grid for Paging Service

Now that we have a BSM for paging services, we are able to begin thinking of how marketing communication can best be used to positively affect the decision to subscribe to a paging service. As always, we need to consider if a single overall message in one primary type of marketing communication will enable us to meet our marketing objectives. In this case, given the two target audience groups, the market-to-market variation, and heavy price competition, an IMC program is necessary, not a simple campaign. Consequently, an IMC Task Grid was developed to help guide the direction of the marketing communications (see Figure 10.9).

Because we are dealing with non-users of a paging service as well as current users, the communication tasks associated with need arousal must address category need. Marketing communication must build the case for more than the brand, it must establish a need for a paging service, and link it to the brand. While this is not necessary for current users, it nonetheless works toward establishing the category need–brand awareness link required for recall-based brand awareness. Along with this task, messages at this stage must facilitate at least an initially positive attitude toward our brand. The best way of accomplishing this is with advertising, and television is ideal for the task.

Figure 10.9
IMC Task Grid for a Paging Service

Decison Stage	Communication Task	Target Audience	Where and When	IMC Options
Need Arousal	Generate interest in paging service among non-users (category need) Stimulate a link between paging service and PAGETIME (brand awareness) Initial positive attitude for our brand (brand attitude)	Current users of a paging service Single adults and families not using a paging service	In home or in conversation after experiencing need to "be in touch"	Television advertising
Check-out Paging Services	Provide easily available information to convince target (brand attitude) Gain positive intention to subscribe to service (brand purchase intention)	Current users of a paging service Single adults and families not using a paging service	In home or in conversations after need arousal Retail outlets	Print advertising Direct mail to trade P-o-p merchandising
Subscribe to Service	Act on positive intention to subscribe (brand purchase intention)	Adult head of household	In home	Advertising Trial promotion
Usage and Reinforcement	Continued use of service (brand purchase intention) Maintain positive attitude toward brand (brand attitude)	Single adults and family members	When used to stay in touch	Direct mail Advertising

Once television advertising has suggested the need for a paging service to non-users, and created awareness of and positive interest in our brand among both non-users and current users of other paging services, these potential triers and switchers move to the next stage of the decision process, check-out paging services. This could begin as soon as the need is aroused, so information or access to sources of information must be readily available. Even current users who become aware of the new paging service may wish to look into it quickly if they are not satisfied with the service they are using. The information provided must be convincing and encourage an intention to subscribe. Advertising-oriented messages are needed here, but broadcast will not do. Print media are appropriate, everything from traditional print advertisements to direct mail to brochures and other point-of-purchase merchandising at retail outlets (if there are any). Potential customers must have time to process and review information at their leisure.

At the subscribe to service stage, we want all those who have considered subscribing to act upon their intention. Here is where the same television advertising that generated the original interest in the brand will help keep both the need, interest, and brand salient in the subscriber's mind. At the same time if a trial promotion is available, this should help finalize the decision. Finally, during the usage and reinforcement stage, direct mail and the ongoing advertising will reinforce the original brand choice and through nurturing a positive attitude toward the service, ensure continued usage of the paging service.

The PAGETIME IMC Program

The specific creative strategy implied by the communication tasks identified in the development of the IMC Task Grid is clearly message oriented, and one that repositions paging services from a business to a personal orientation. The Primary Creative Brief used to guide the creative execution is shown in Figure 10.10. The creative task outlined in the first four sections of the brief focuses upon the need to deal effectively with the two distinct target audience groups. We know from the thinking that went into developing the BSM that different messages, and hence different creative briefs, for each group are not necessary. The decision process in selecting a paging service is the same for both first-time triers and potential switchers. The key for non-users is arousing need, but this attention to category need is also a plus for attracting switchers as well because it forges a link between the need for a paging service and PAGETIME. With need established among non-users, we want both groups to select PAGETIME.

Figure 10.10
Primary Creative Brief for PAGETIME

PRODUCT PAGETIME	JOB	DATE
KEY MARKET OBSERVATIONS Significant differences in paging service penetration between and within markets; very price competitive		
SOURCE OF BUSINESS New category users and switchers from competitive services		
CONSUMER BARRIER/INSIGHT Even among non-users of paging services there is interest in a service that would promote greater peace-of-mind and less anxiety over missing important communication if the cost was less than $10/month		
TARGET MARKET Families and individuals 18 through 55 with active lifestyles		
COMMUNICATION OBJECTIVES AND TASKS Category need–brand awareness link and positive brand attitude based upon meaningful difference		
BRAND ATTITUDE STRATEGY High involvement/informational brand strategy driven by problem avoidance and incomplete satisfaction motives		
BENEFIT CLAIM AND SUPPORT PAGETIME helps you stay in touch affordably. Support: paging fits your lifestyle and is only $8.95 per month		
DESIRED CONSUMER RESPONSE Non-users recognize paging is not just for business, but for them; both users and switchers see PAGETIME as a good value		
CREATIVE GUIDELINES Utilized lifestyle vignettes that "fit" target audience and maintain consistent look and feel while tailoring messages to specific market requirements		
REQUIREMENTS/MANDATORY CONTENT Match service detail to market		

The objectives and strategy detailed in the next four sections of the Primary Creative Brief provide an overview of how the creative executions will meet these communication tasks. The real strategic key is the repositioning of the category to personal use. Not only does this open up the category for non-users, but it offers a unique and differentiating position for the brand that sets it apart from competitors in the minds of current users of other paging services. This important distinction aids salience for PAGETIME, and encourages potential switchers to think about the brand. The "affordable" support provides the necessary element for convincing both target groups that PAGETIME is the best paging service for their lifestyle needs.

The actual executions utilize lifestyle vignettes that reflect easily recognized situations from the lives of the target audience, and this visual imagery is used to provide consistency between executions. This is readily apparent in looking at two of the direct mail brochures (Figure 10.11) and frames from the television advertising (Figure 10.12). Here we can see how a consistent look and feel exists between the two brochures, as well as

Figure 10.11
PAGETIME Direct Mail Brochures

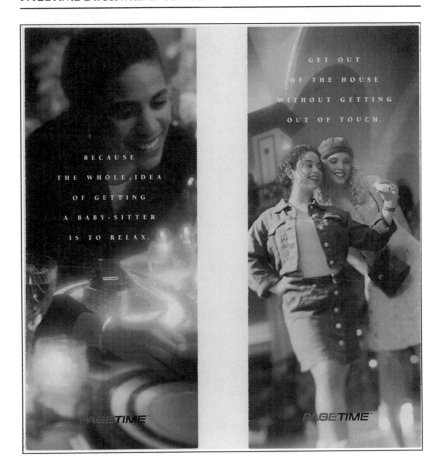

Figure 10.12
PAGETIME Television Commercial That Carries Over the Look and Feel of Print Ads

a carryover between the print and television. In fact, the same images were used in all of PAGETIME's marketing communication. This is made possible by IMC; a central responsibility for marketing communication planning.

IMC Media Budget Allocation Grid

The actual implementation of the PAGETIME IMC campaign that resulted from this strategic planning can be seen in the IMC Media Budget Allocation Grid shown in Figure 10.13. In reviewing the implementation of this IMC program we must bear two points in mind: the unique relationships between PAGETIME and Adelphia Cable and the significant market-to-market differences.

It was mentioned earlier that Adelphia Cable was in effect the marketing arm for PAGETIME. Because PAGETIME is a part of Adelphia Cable, it has direct access via run-of-schedule programming on cable networks (e.g., CNN, USA, TNT, and Lifetime) to cable-wired homes in their markets, as well as a direct mail link via the monthly cable bill. For this reason, given the heavy penetration of cable in PAGETIME's market and the strong correlation between cable subscribers and paging service interest, PAGETIME is using Adelphia Cable subscribers as the market for their introduction. This decision was made for the obvious reason of media delivery efficiency, but as importantly, because television is clearly the best IMC option for the critical category need and brand awareness objectives, and direct mail offers an excellent means of targeting the delivery of the message needed to satisfy the brand attitude and brand purchase intention communication objectives. Adelphia Cable offices, where customers come for information and to pay cable bills, also provided an ideal merchandising opportunity.

Because of the significant difference in paging service penetration between (and within) markets, while the same IMC media options are used in each market, it is possible to vary the message in each market if necessary. While each market receives the same primary message, details such as the calling area coverage naturally differ. This is why direct mail is more effective than other forms of print advertising (although newspaper could be an alternative, albeit less targeted). It also provides the option of much more targeted promotions to accommodate trial versus switching incentives. For example, in low-penetration areas a trial promotion featuring a significant savings or a free pager would make sense, while in high-penetration areas a promotion featuring free activation to the PAGETIME frequency could be used.

PAGETIME has been able to apply IMC strategic planning to a potentially complicated marketing communication problem, and through that planning effect an efficient IMC program.

Figure 10.13
IMC Media Budget Allocation Grid for PAGETIME

IMC Communication Options	Communication Tasks				
	Generate Interest in Paging Service	Provide Link between Paging Service and PAGETIME and Create Tentative Interest	Provide Information to Convince	Seek Positive Intent	Continued Usage
Primary: television advertising					
direct mail	■				
Secondary: trial promotion	■	■	■		■
p-o-p	■				

Transitions Comfort Lenses

Our final IMC application really underscores the importance and power of good strategic integrated marketing communications planning. Transitions Comfort Lenses are a recent innovation in plastic lenses for eyewear, the first viable plastic photochromic (changes with the light) lenses. Introduced nationally by Transitions Optical, Inc. (a division of PPG Industries and Essilor) in 1995, what made it such a marketing challenge was its dependence upon *two* primary target audiences.

With almost any product or service, the trade is an important part of the marketing program. But rarely is the trade also an integral part of the *consumer's* decision process. However, such is the case with eyecare products. An eyecare professional prescribes lenses for the patient, and at the same time also represents the "trade" for such products. They are the retail distributors. As a result, they must make decisions about what products they will dispense, with both practice management and patient considerations in mind. This means they must carry the brand, much as any brand must be stocked if it is to be purchased, but they also participate in the patient's decision, for they must prescribe the lenses.

We shall see as we get into this example, that in a very real sense the decision process involved is itself integrated. It requires "push" on the part of the eyecare professional and "pull" on the part of the patient. An overview of this decision process is outlined in Figure 10.14. Initially, eyecare professionals must become aware of the new lens, and consider how it may or may not fit within their practice. Once accepted, it must be recommended to patients—the "push." At the same time, patients with an interest or need for tinted lenses of some kind must be made aware of the

---

Figure 10.14
Overview of Prescription Eyeglass Lens Decision Process

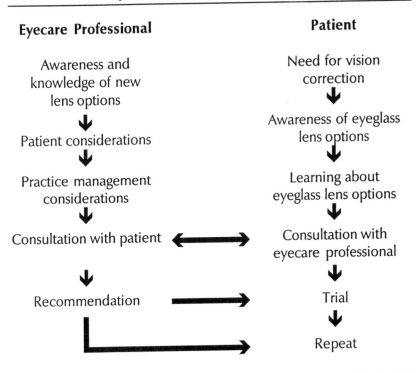

Eyecare Professional	Patient
Awareness and knowledge of new lens options	Need for vision correction
↓	↓
Patient considerations	Awareness of eyeglass lens options
↓	↓
Practice management considerations	Learning about eyeglass lens options
↓	↓
Consultation with patient ⟷	Consultation with eyecare professional
↓	↓
Recommendation ⟶	Trial
⌐⟶	↓
	Repeat

---

new lens and learn about its advantages over other alternatives. Then, when consulting their eyecare professional, they inquire about the lenses—the "pull." It is certainly true that in one sense there really is no need for the "pull" of consumer demand. If the eyecare professional is convinced of the lens' value, it will be recommended in any event. But the value of involving the patient, from Transitions' point of view, is that it will make the sale from such a recommendation easier, and also helps ensure the eyecare professionals will carry the lens because of the demand (always assuming it meets their professional standards).

Marketing Background

Answers to the questions posed by the Marketing Background Worksheet provide a good understanding of the problems that confronted Transitions Optical in their introduction of the Comfort Lens.

Product Description. What is being marketed? As already described, the product is a plastic photochromic lens for eyeglasses. But the key here is that the product is the first viable *plastic* photochromic lens. Glass photochromic lenses had been available for 25 years. Plastic lenses, of course, are significantly lighter than glass lenses.

Market Assessment. What is the overall assessment of the market where the product competes? The overall retail optical market is huge, a $12.9 billion industry. Within the tinted lenses sub-market, however, there was a reservoir of negative experiences with glass photochromic lenses among both users and eyecare professionals. Additionally, there is a great deal of general retail optical media clutter that must be contended with; upwards of $200 million directed toward consumers.

Source of Business. Where is the business expected to come from? At a macro level, all wearers of prescription eyeglasses are part of the market, but more specifically business is expected to come from those with particular sensitivities to light and glare, and those who currently utilize some form of tinted or photochromic lens. Because this is a new product with a distinct advantage over glass photochromic lenses, Transitions Comfort Lenses are expected to grow the market for photochromic lenses.

Competitive Evaluation. How does the competition position itself? Traditional glass photochromic lenses are positioned strictly against the functional attribute of changing tint with changes in light. But as just noted, there are established *negative* perceptions of photochromic lenses among both patients and eyecare professionals. Corning PhotoGray glass photochromic lenses had defined the category for decades, and were perceived as an "old" product. Additionally, Transitions can expect competition from new direct competition, especially a number of Japanese companies, just entering the plastic photochromics market.

Marketing Objectives. What are the marketing objectives for Transitions Comfort Lenses? The specific marketing objectives are to increase retail sales of Transitions Comfort Lenses by a specific percentage (based upon test market results), and to increase national market share points from pre-marketing communication levels.

Marketing Communication. How is marketing communication expected to contribute to the marketing objective? The key here is to not only raise awareness of the brand, but to create positive attitudes toward *plastic* photochromic lenses and the brand, overcoming existing negative attitudes toward current photochromic lenses. This requires effort against both consumer and trade.

Target Audience

We have already seen that Transitions Comfort Lenses has the unique challenge of satisfying two primary target audiences. This leads to a rather complex target audience definition, as answers to the Key Target Audience Worksheet Questions make clear.

Where are sales or usage to come from—customers or non-customers? Since we are dealing with a new product, as well as a new category for the manufacturer, we are dealing with non-customers at both the trade and consumer level, at least initially.

Does the marketing objective involve initiating trial or continued usage? Again, because we are dealing with a new product, trial is essential. But to satisfy the marketing objective, there must also be repeat purchase objectives for the trade. While we certainly want to lay the foundation for continued usage by patients who try Transitions Comfort Lenses, given the likely purchase cycle for eyeglasses, this would not be an objective in this first year.

Where does the trade fit? The trade, the eyecare professional, is an integral part of the consumer's, or patient's, decision to try the product. In this case, the eyecare professional must be treated both as part of the distribution system, a traditional trade role, as well as perhaps the key influencer, or even decider, in the consumer decision process. It is in this latter role or roles that the eyecare professional must be considered part of the primary target audience.

What do we know about the target audience? Demographic information suggests the consumer target audience is adult eyeglass wearers 35 to 64 years of age in households with incomes of $30,000 or more. But importantly we also know they may be described as generally active, with a busy lifestyle, looking for comfort and convenience in the products they use. The trade component of the target audience takes in all eyecare professionals associated with the retail optical market. Additionally, both the consumer and trade are skeptical about claims for new eyeglass lenses, and have negative attitudes about existing photochromic lens products. This last point is a critical consideration, because negative attitudes always override positive ones in decision making. Therefore, this must be addressed.

Whom are the decision makers the marketing communications must reach? We have already noted that both the eyecare professional and the patient will be decision makers, and play various roles in the decision process. Normally when one completes a Decision Grid, the various roles played by the consumer and trade reflect the traditional distinction between the two groups. In this case, as we consider the Decision Grid it is important to remember that the patient and eyecare professional are working together to arrive at a decision, and that the roles each play are often interchangeable. For example, the eyecare professional may initiate interest on the part of the patient for Transitions Comfort Lenses, but it may equally be the case that the patient initiates interest for the eyecare professional by asking questions about the product.

Decision Grid

People who might play a role in a patient's decision to purchase Transitions Comfort Lenses are listed in the Decision Grid shown in Figure 10.15, and the thinking behind their consideration is reviewed below.

Initiator: Who is likely to initiate interest in plastic photochromic lenses? Obviously the patient or the eyecare professional might make the first suggestion. But, so too might other family members or friends. At the very least, there are two "audiences" likely to play an initiating role at the beginning of the decision process.

Influencer: Once initial interest has been aroused, who is likely to have any influence on the decision? Again, the patient and the eyecare professional certainly, and possibly other family members or friends. When is this

Figure 10.15

Transitions Comfort Lenses Consumer Decision Grid

	Target Audience	
Role	**Consumer**	**Trade**
Initiator	patient family friends	eyecare professional
Influencer	patient family friends	eyecare professional
Decider	patient family	eyecare professional
Purchaser	patient	
User	patient	eyecare professional

influence most likely to occur in the decision process? Because the purchase of a new type of eyeglass lens is most likely a high involvement decision, there will be some kind of information search and evaluation stage in the decision process as the potential user forms attitudes about the positive and negative aspects of the product. If this were a low involvement decision, there would be no need for information search and evaluation, and influence would occur when category need was felt. This will be an important consideration when roles are reevaluated for future campaigns and repeat purchase becomes important.

Decider: When it comes to the actual decision, who is most likely to participate? Once again the patient and eyecare professional, but what about others? Friends would no longer be involved, but in the case of teenagers and/or younger children, the parent would almost certainly be involved in the decision. In high involvement decisions, the resolution to buy is usually made ahead of the actual time of purchase, in which case the deciders will probably form an intention to buy at the tail-end of their evaluation of the product. An actual final decision would then come later, at the point of purchase. But given the unique interaction between the patient and eyecare professional, this could (and probably often will) occur all at the point of purchase. Where and when these roles are played are carefully considered in the development of the Behavioral Sequence Model.

Purchaser: The actual purchase will be effected by the patient; or in certain other cases (e.g., with teens), someone else in the family. Obviously, this role is played at the point of purchase.

User: Finally, the patient is, of course, the user of the new Transitions Comfort Lenses, but not the only person concerned with usage. The eyecare professional must retain confidence in his or her recommendation, and will monitor the suitability of the lenses.

Communication Strategy

From the marketing background and target audience information, we are now able to begin outlining a communication strategy. The three key Communication Strategy Worksheet questions help us define what we hope to accomplish with our communication efforts in support of the Transitions Comfort Lenses marketing objectives.

What are the communication objectives? We know that brand awareness and brand attitude are always communication objectives. In this case, because we are dealing with a new product, awareness will be critical. But whether the brand awareness objective should be recognition or recall is not straightforward. In fact, this is one of those infrequent times when both recognition- and recall-based brand awareness will be operating. For most people, the dominant form of awareness will be recall: the need for new eyeglasses will trigger awareness of Transitions Comfort lenses. But for others, it will be recognition. This will be especially true for patients who have not formed specific attitudes, but are reminded of the brand when it is recommended by an eyecare professional.

The brand attitude objective will need to deal with the negative prior attitudes toward photochromic lenses, especially among eyecare professionals. This negative attitude suggests category need must also be a communication objective. Ordinarily, a product like Transitions Comfort Lenses would be considered a "new-and-improved" photochromic lens. It is that, but because of the problems associated with traditional glass photochromic lenses (things like weight and speed of lens color change), emphasis must be placed upon these plastic lenses as defining a new category without the negative baggage of the old category. One final communication objective for eyecare professionals, of course, is brand purchase intention. The trade must carry the lenses.

What is the brand attitude strategy? The brand attitude strategy for Transitions Comfort Lenses is high involvement/informational. The nature of the decision is high involvement for several reasons. It is a new product attempting to define a new category, replacing old products that have perceived problems. It is an infrequently purchased product by the patient, not inexpensive, and needed to correct or aid vision. For the eyecare professional, a recommendation reflects professional reputation and expertise. Clearly there is risk attached to this decision for both the patient and eyecare professional.

The underlying motivation in the decision is negative, hence an informational strategy. The most likely motivation is problem-solution or incomplete satisfaction. The assumption here is that normal lenses or glass photochromics do not adequately address issues important to the patient (which would equally serve as the motivation for the eyecare professional).

What do we want people to do as a result of our communication? Specifically, we want both consumers and trade to become familiar with Transitions Comfort Lenses, and form positive attitudes about them. These positive attitudes will be based upon information that will help reposition Transitions Comfort Lenses away from traditional glass photochromic lenses. As a result of this information, we expect to stimulate interest on the part of the patient and actual stocking and recommendation to their patients by eyecare professionals.

Constructing a Behavioral Sequence Model

We know that the decision involved in purchasing or prescribing Transitions Comfort Lenses is high involvement. This means that the appropriate BSM will reflect the generic high involvement model: need arousal, information search and evaluation, purchase, and usage. But because of research that was conducted, a more detailed understanding of the decision process involved was available (as we saw reflected in Figure 10.14). Given this understanding, the following four decision stages were used in constructing the BSM for the consumer: awareness of needs and options, learning about options, consultation/recommendation, and usage and reinforcement (Figure 10.16).

Awareness of Needs and Options. In this first stage of the decision process, all of the potential participants in the decision will play a role as possibly an initiator or influencer: the eyecare professional, patient, family, and friends. They may learn about it almost anywhere after the national introduction in 1995: at home or work, when talking with others or through some kind of marketing communication. (The eyecare professional will, of course, have an opportunity of hearing about Transitions Comfort Lenses through trade sources, but we are only considering them here in

Figure 10.16

Consumer BSM for Transitions Comfort Lenses

Consideration at Each Stage	Decision Stage			
	Awareness of Need and Options	Learning about Options	Consultation/ Recommendation	Usage and Reinforcement
Decision roles involved	Eyecare professional as initiator/ influencer Patient, family members, friends, as initiator/ influencer	Eyecare professional as influencer Patient, family members as influencer/ decider Friends as influencer	Eyecare professional as influencer/ decider Patient, adult family members as influencer/ decider	Patient as user/decider Eyecare professional as influencer/ decider
Where stage is likely to occur	In home In office Retail outlet Marketing communication	In home In office Retail outlet Marketing communication	Office Retail outlet	When wearing glasses Eyecare professional's office or retail outlet Marketing communication
Timing of stage	1995 national launch	Ongoing	Ongoing	After purchase
How it is likely to occur	Patient notices vision problems All hear about/read about new plastic photochromic Transitions Comfort Lenses	All seek information about new Transitions Comfort Lenses	Patient (family) consults with eyecare professional Eyecare professional recommends Transitions Comfort Lenses	Patient tries Eyecare professional monitors usage

their roles as part of the *patient's* purchase decision. There is, of course, a separate BSM for the decision to purchase and dispense Transitions Comfort Lenses, which will be discussed shortly.)

Learning about Options. All of the potential participants in the first stage are also likely to play a role in this second stage as well, but their roles will be different. The eyecare professional has an opportunity to influence the decision at this stage, as do friends. The patient and patient's family will also play an influencer role, but they will also play a role as decider. While the final decision is not likely at this stage, intentions will begin to form. All of this will come about as the participants learn about Transitions Comfort Lenses through a variety of sources.

Consultation/Recommendation. The actual decision to try Transitions Comfort Lenses will be made in the eyecare professional's office or retail store. The eyecare professional will continue in the role of influencer, but may also play a deciding role as well. The patient (or adult family member if the patient is a younger child) will be the principal decider, and will be the purchaser.

Usage and Reinforcement. After purchase, it is the patient alone in the role of user. But during this stage the patient will also continue to play the role of decider, evaluating the performance of the lenses. The eyecare professional too will play a decider role at this stage, along with continuing to be an influencer. This will occur during checkups. Marketing communication, for example ongoing advertising or point-of-purchase merchandising, will help keep the brand name salient, and reinforce positive attitudes.

Trade BSM

While the eyecare professional is a significant part of the consumer's decision process, they also constitute the majority of the trade in the more traditional sense. Because much of the marketing communication effort to the trade will influence the eyecare professional's participation in the consumer's decision process, there is a need for a high degree of congruence between trade and consumer messages. This is yet another reason why IMC is so critical to Transitions Comfort Lenses. Figure 10.17 provides the BSM for the trade aspect of the eyecare professional's decision.

As you can see, the stages reflect the high involvement nature of this decision: awareness of new options, learning about new options, practice management consideration, and acquisition/review. It should also be clear that the first two stages correspond to the eyecare professional's participation in the consumer's decision process. The difference is that this trade BSM accounts for the roles other people involved with the eyecare

Figure 10.17

Trade BSM for Transitions Comfort Lenses

Consideration at Each Stage	Decision Stage			
	Awareness of New Options	Learning about New Options	Practice Management Communication	Acquisition/ Review
Decision roles involved	Salespeople as initiator Colleagues as initiator/ influencer Eyecare professionals as initiator/ influencer	Salespeople as influencer Colleagues as influencer/ decider Eyecare professional as influencer/ decider	Colleagues as influencer/ decider Eyecare professional as decider	Eyecare professional as decider/ purchaser/user
Where stage is likely to occur	Office or retail outlet Trade shows Conferences Marketing communication	Office or retail outlet Trade shows Conferences Marketing communication	Office or retail outlet	Office or retail outlet
Timing of stage	1995 national launch	Ongoing	After learning and trial	Ongoing
How it is likely to occur	Eyecare professional hears about new plastic photochromic lenses/ Transitions Comfort Lenses	Seeks information about new lenses/ Transitions Comfort Lenses Assesses likely peformance	Assesses likely patient interest and need Assesses revenue potential	Initial trial of Transitions Comfort Lenses Review of potential patient satisfaction

professional play in raising awareness of Transitions Comfort Lenses, and providing relevant information. The third stage reflects consideration outside of those directly related to the patient, those things that affect the practice itself. The last stage reflects the decision to include Transitions Comfort Lenses in the practice, and the ongoing review of the product's contribution both to the patient and the practice.

IMC Task Grid

All of the IMC Planning Worksheets are now completed and the appropriate BSMs have been developed. There is no doubt that a single message directed at one primary target audience, using one primary type of marketing communication, would never be able to do the job necessary to accomplish Transitions Comfort Lenses' marketing objectives. This is an obvious case for IMC. In fact, as we have seen, it is a very complicated marketing communication problem calling for careful IMC strategic planning. Working through an IMC Task Grid helps us to effectively plan the IMC program.

The IMC Task Grid details the specific results expected from marketing communications at each stage of the decision process, whom should be targeted, and the best way of reaching them. While the BSM suggests that family and friends can often participate as initiators and influencers in the decision, they are not a primary target audience. We will only be directly addressing the patient and eyecare professional in our effort to affect consumer decision making. The IMC Task Grid for the consumer is shown in Figure 10.18.

Awareness of Need and Options. Patients must be made aware of this new category of eyeglass lenses, *plastic* lenses that adjust to any light, and interest stimulated in Transitions Comfort Lenses. The best way of driving awareness is with traditional advertising, especially television. The eyecare professional too must be made aware of these new lenses, along with a preliminary understanding of its performance characteristics, in order to stimulate interest in looking further. These messages can be communicated by advertising in both professional journals and trade publications.

Learning about Options. At the second stage, the most logical place for a patient to seek information is from his or her eyecare professional, so it will be necessary for brochures and other information to be available at the eyecare professional's office or retail outlet. Additionally, advertising should continue to provide information, especially at the early stages of interest. An important communication task at this stage will be to relate the properties of these new lenses to perceived need. In this case, that means that the ability to adjust to any light and the lighter weight of plastic contribute to the patient's desire for total comfort in prescription lenses.

For the eyecare professional, it will be necessary to educate and build a favorable attitude toward Transitions Comfort Lenses by discussing patient consideration as well as product performance. This is especially true

Figure 10.18

Transitions Comfort Lenses Consumer IMC Task Grid

Decison Stage	Communication Task	Target Audience	Where and When	IMC Options
Awareness of Needs and Options	Category awareness: *plastic* lenses that adjust to any light (category need) Awareness of Transitions Comfort Lenses (recall and recognition awareness)	Current prescription eyeglass wearer Eyecare professional	In home Eyecare professional office or retail outlet	Consumer advertising (broadcast and print) Trade advertising
Learning about Options	Provide enough information to convince consumer target (brand attitude) Provide enough information on both product and patient consideration to convince trade target (brand attitude)	Current prescription eyeglass wearer Eyecare professional	In home Eyecare professional office or retail outlet	Print advertising (consumer and trade) Point-of-purchase Direct mail to trade Trade shows
Consultation/ Recommendation	Gain positive intention (brand purchase intention) Act on positive intention (brand attitude and brand purchase intention)	Current prescription eyeglass wearer Eyecare professional	Eyecare professional office or retail outlet	Point-of-purchase
Usage and Reinforcement	Reinforce decision (brand attitude and brand purchase intention)	Transitions Comfort Lens user Eyecare professional	When wearing lenses Eyecare professional's office or retail outlet	Co-op advertising Trade advertising

given the residual negative attitudes associated with the traditional photo-chromic lenses. These messages can be communicated via trade advertising, trade shows, and direct mail programs.

Consultation/Recommendation. To facilitate the actual purchase, the patient must consult with an eyecare professional and try the product. This requires good point-of-purchase material at the eyecare professional's office or retail store. At this point in the decision process, the eyecare professional will need to feel comfortable in communicating his or her recommendation, and the point-of-purchase material will help accomplish this.

Usage and Reinforcement. Once the patient has purchased Transitions Comfort Lenses, it will be necessary to reinforce confidence in the decision. Here again traditional advertising helps give the patient the comfort of feeling a part of a much wider group of users than may actually be the case. Using co-op advertising where the eyecare professional is able to "tag" his or her association with the lenses helps to reinforce the eyecare professional's link to the patient's decision. This also helps reinforce the eyecare professional's decision to dispense the product. Additionally, this message can be communicated to the eyecare professional through professional journal and trade publication advertising.

Trade IMC Task Grid

Since the first two stages of the trade BSM are the same for the eyecare professional as the consumer BSM, they have already been addressed (salespeople are not part of our target audience, and colleagues are in fact eyecare professionals). However, the last two stages of the trade BSM for the eyecare professional do differ from the decision processes involved when they are part of the consumer's BSM.

Practice Management Considerations. Independent of satisfying patient needs, eyecare professionals must also be attentive to the impact of what they dispense in their practices. A key concern is patient demand, and a merchandiser program to acquaint eyecare professionals with the consumer IMC "pull" support would address that issue. Additionally, co-op advertising programs help associate the eyecare professional's specific practice with Transitions Comfort Lenses.

Acquisitions/Review. In this last stage of the trade decision, incentives can be offered to help initiate trial, while general consumer and trade advertising will continue to reinforce the decision.

The Transitions Comfort Lenses IMC Program

With the completion of the IMC Task Grids, Transitions Optical has a blueprint for implementing a truly effective IMC program for introducing Transitions Comfort Lenses. A review of the task grids suggests that the primary thrust of the IMC campaign should be message-oriented, although promotions will play an important part. This means that a Primary Creative Brief must be prepared with advertising in mind. (See Figure 10.19.)

Based upon this IMC planning, it was decided that consumer advertising should be the primary IMC option, primarily because it would facilitate the first two stages of the decision process for both the patient and the eyecare professional. Both print and television advertising were created, with allowance made in the television for a dealer co-op tag (see Figures 10.20 and 10.21 for examples). The secondary IMC options (still within the outline of the Primary Communication Creative Brief, as discussed in Chapter 4) included direct mail to eyecare professionals and point-of-purchase merchandising material for use in the eyecare professional's office or retail store (see Figure 10.22a and 10.22b for an example of a p-o-p brochure and rack).

We talked in Chapter 4 about the need for a consistent look and feel to all elements of an IMC campaign. Utilizing general creative briefs helps accomplish this, and this is well illustrated in the examples shown here (as it was in all of the material produced). In each of the executions the viewer or reader receives a "point of view" look at the product. One is able to "see" the lens in action (a strong key to effective communication); in effect a demonstration of the lenses, even in print. This device not only has the advantage of tying together all of the executions with the desired look and feel, it communicates the product's primary attribute (comfort via sensitivity to light changes), and helps establish the new category–brand awareness link. If all of this work had not been centrally managed within an IMC context, what do you think the likelihood would have been that all of these creative executions would have worked together?

To accommodate the specific needs of the eyecare professional, those that went beyond their participation in the patient's decision process, a Secondary Creative Brief was developed to help guide the additional creative work for the trade. This included print advertising to the trade, direct

Figure 10.19
Primary Communication Creative Brief for Transitions Comfort Lenses

PRODUCT Transitions Comfort Lenses	JOB	DATE

KEY MARKET OBSERVATIONS
Consumer research identified the importance of "comfort" in the selection of eyewear, and importantly that "comfort" includes how well they can see with the glasses

SOURCE OF BUSINESS
Current prescription eyeglass wearers

CONSUMER INSIGHT
Residual negative attitudes toward traditional photochromic lenses

TARGET MARKET
Adult eyeglass wearers and eyecare professionals

COMMUNICATION OBJECTIVES AND TASKS
Brand awareness within a primary brand attitude objective that equates "comfort" with the new lenses

BRAND ATTITUDE STRATEGY
High involvement/informational brand strategy driven by motivations of problem-solution and incomplete satisfaction

BENEFIT CLAIM AND SUPPORT
Transitions Comfort Lenses are comfortable. Support: They lighten and darken as light changes and are lightweight plastic prescription lenses

DESIRED CONSUMER RESPONSE
Believe that lenses that are light-sensitive will mean visual comfort and try them

CREATIVE GUIDELINES
Demonstrate tint change effect

REQUIREMENTS/MANDATORY CONTENT
None

mail, incentive promotions, and trade shows. In addition, a specific effort was made to merchandise to the trade the consumer advertising program to help satisfy the practice management consideration stage of their decision (an example is shown in Figure 10.23). All of this material, of course, was consistent with the overall look and feel of the primary creative because of the centrally managed development of the IMC program.

Figure 10.20
Transitions Comfort Lenses Television Commercial with Dealer Tag Allowance

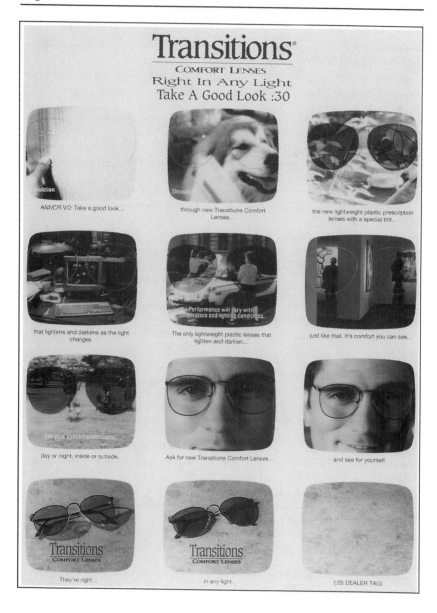

Figure 10.21
Transitions Comfort Lenses Print Ad

Figure 10.22a
P-o-p Brochure Rack for Transitions Comfort Lenses

Figure 10.22b
P-o-p Brochure for Transitions Comfort Lenses

Figure 10.23
Trade Ad for Transitions Comfort Lenses

IMC Media Budget Allocation Grid

The choice of media for the consumer portion of the Transitions Comfort Lenses IMC program is shown in the IMC Budget Allocation Grid illustrated in Figure 10.24. What it reveals is a good example of how IMC enables a marketer to maximize the strengths of various media in satisfying communication objectives. The brand awareness communication objective for Transitions Comfort Lenses is primarily recall, but we have seen that there is also a component of recognition. Television is the best medium for driving both types of brand awareness. While magazines have a frequency limitation for recall awareness, it is fine for recognition; newspapers have a potential color limitation for recognition awareness, but no recall limitation. By using the two together there is adequate reinforcement for both the recognition and recall brand awareness objectives.

Point-of-purchase and direct mail have limitations associated with brand awareness, but these are mediated by their use as secondary media. Point-of-purchase and direct mail require prior exposure to the brand if they are to contribute to recognition awareness, and the primary media provide that exposure. Direct mail is limited by its low frequency for recall, but again the primary media help provide frequency. While point-of-purchase generally is not appropriate for recall awareness (and much of the merchandising material created, such as posters and flip-charts for use by the eyecare professional, are not meant to be, but are used in patient consultation), the brochures offered are used by patients in learning about Transitions Comfort Lenses, and likely to be taken home. Taken together, the creativity that was developed and the media selected for delivering it do an excellent job in satisfying the brand awareness communication objective.

Looking at the brand attitude communication objective, again we can see how the IMC media selected work together to satisfy the high involvement/informational strategy. We know that television alone is inappropriate for high involvement informational decisions because there is not enough time to process the information necessary to convince. But used in conjunction with print advertising that does provide enough detail, a synergy is created between the actual demonstration that television is able to show of the lenses changing tint in response to light changes in a wearer's environment and the "static" demonstration in print. Among the secondary media, direct mail does a good job of meeting the objectives for the eyecare professional, and the point-of-purchase, which is often limited by a lack of processing time, does not suffer that limitation in this case because it is being used at the learning about options and consultation/recommendation stages of the decision when time *will* be taken with the material (unlike most retail point-of-purchase, where the average decision time is less than 10 seconds).

Figure 10.24

Transitions Comfort Lenses IMC Consumer Media Budget Allocation Grid

IMC Communication Options	Communication Tasks				
	Create Category and Brand Awareness	Provide Information to Convince	Seek Positive Intent	Action on Intent	Reinforce Decision
Primary: television advertising			■	■	
magazine advertising				■	
newspaper insert				■	
Secondary: p-o-p	■				
direct mail	■				■

What we have seen in this Transitions Comfort Lenses example is how IMC planning was able to effectively deal with a very complicated decision process involving consumers and trade in not only their traditional, independent decisions (consumers to try and use a product and the trade to provide it), but interacting as well. This simply could not have been done as effectively without IMC planning. It was the careful attention to these intersecting creative needs through a variety of media that made this campaign work. The marketing objectives were not only met; they were exceeded. This could only have been accomplished by centrally managing and understanding the entire marketing communication effort. This is what IMC is all about.

The illustrations in this book appear courtesy of the following sources:

Figures 2.4, 2.5, 2.6, 10.4, 10.5, and 10.6 courtesy of Lichtwer Pharma U.S., Inc. Figures 10.11 and 10.12 courtesy of PAGETIME. Figures 10.20, 10.21, 10.22a, 10.22b, and 10.23, courtesy of Transitions Optical.

INDEX

American Marketing Association

———

As a marketing professional or student you'll never get enough information about marketing.

One way to stay up-to-date with the latest academic theories, the war stories, the global techniques, and the leading technologies is to become a member of the American Marketing Association.

For a free membership information kit
phone: 312-648-0536,
FAX: 312-993-7542,
or write to the American Marketing Association at 250 S. Wacker Drive, Chicago, Illinois 60606.

TITLES OF INTEREST IN MARKETING, DIRECT MARKETING, AND SALES PROMOTION

SUCCESSFUL DIRECT MARKETING METHODS, by Bob Stone
PROFITABLE DIRECT MARKETING, by Jim Kobs
INTEGRATED DIRECT MARKETING, by Ernan Roman
BEYOND 2000: THE FUTURE OF DIRECT MARKETING, by Jerry I. Reitman
POWER DIRECT MARKETING, by "Rocket" Ray Jutkins
CREATIVE STRATEGY IN DIRECT MARKETING, by Susan K. Jones
SECRETS OF SUCCESSFUL DIRECT MAIL, by Richard V. Benson
STRATEGIC DATABASE MARKETING, by Rob Jackson and Paul Wang
HOW TO PROFIT THROUGH CATALOG MARKETING, by Katie Muldoon
DIRECT RESPONSE TELEVISION, by Frank Brady and J. Angel Vasquez
DIRECT MARKETING THROUGH BROADCAST MEDIA, by Alvin Eicoff
SUCCESSFUL TELEMARKETING, by Bob Stone and John Wyman
BUSINESS TO BUSINESS DIRECT MARKETING, by Robert Bly
COMMONSENSE DIRECT MARKETING, by Drayton Bird
DIRECT MARKETING CHECKLISTS, by John Stockwell and Henry Shaw
INTEGRATED MARKETING COMMUNICATIONS, by Don E. Schultz, Stanley I. Tannenbaum,
    and Robert F. Lauterborn
GREEN MARKETING, by Jacquelyn Ottman
MARKETING CORPORATE IMAGE: THE COMPANY AS YOUR NUMBER ONE PRODUCT
    by James R. Gregory with Jack G. Wiechmann
HOW TO CREATE SUCCESSFUL CATALOGS, by Maxwell Sroge
101 TIPS FOR MORE PROFITABLE CATALOGS, by Maxwell Sroge
SALES PROMOTION ESSENTIALS
    by Don E. Schultz, William A. Robinson and Lisa A. Petrison
PROMOTIONAL MARKETING, by William A. Robinson and Christine Hauri
BEST SALES PROMOTIONS, by William A. Robinson
INSIDE THE LEADING MAIL ORDER HOUSES, by Maxwell Sroge
NEW PRODUCT DEVELOPMENT, by George Gruenwald
NEW PRODUCT DEVELOPMENT CHECKLISTS, by George Gruenwald
CLASSIC FAILURES IN PRODUCT MARKETING, by Donald W. Hendon
HOW TO TURN CUSTOMER SERVICE INTO CUSTOMER SALES, by Bernard Katz
ADVERTISING & MARKETING CHECKLISTS, by Ron Kaatz
BRAND MARKETING, by William M. Weilbacher
MARKETING WITHOUT MONEY, by Nicholas E. Bade
THE 1-DAY MARKETING PLAN, by Roman A. Hiebing, Jr. and Scott W. Cooper
HOW TO WRITE A SUCCESSFUL MARKETING PLAN
    by Roman G. Hiebing, Jr. and Scott W. Cooper
DEVELOPING, IMPLEMENTING, AND MANAGING EFFECTIVE MARKETING PLANS
    by Hal Goetsch
HOW TO EVALUATE AND IMPROVE YOUR MARKETING DEPARTMENT
    by Keith Sparling and Gerard Earls
SELLING TO A SEGMENTED MARKET, by Chester A. Swenson
MARKET-ORIENTED PRICING, by Michael Morris and Gene Morris
STATE-OF-THE-ART MARKETING RESEARCH, by A.B. Blankenship and George E. Breen
AMA HANDBOOK FOR CUSTOMER SATISFACTION, by Alan Dutka
WAS THERE A PEPSI GENERATION BEFORE PEPSI DISCOVERED IT?
    by Stanley C. Hollander and Richard Germain
BUSINESS TO BUSINESS COMMUNICATIONS HANDBOOK, by Fred Messner
MANAGING SALES LEADS: HOW TO TURN EVERY PROSPECT INTO A CUSTOMER
    by Robert Donath, Richard Crocker, Carol Dixon and James Obermeyer
AMA MARKETING TOOLBOX (SERIES), by David Parmerlee
AMA COMPLETE GUIDE TO SMALL BUSINESS MARKETING, by Kenneth J. Cook
AMA COMPLETE GUIDE TO STRATEGIC PLANNING FOR SMALL BUSINESS, by Kenneth J. Cook
AMA COMPLETE GUIDE TO SMALL BUSINESS ADVERTISING, by Joe Vitale
HOW TO GET THE MOST OUT OF TRADE SHOWS, by Steve Miller
HOW TO GET THE MOST OUT OF SALES MEETINGS, by James Dance
STRATEGIC MARKET PLANNING, by Robert J. Hamper and L. Sue Baugh

For further information or a current catalog, write:
NTC Business Books
a division of NTC *Publishing Group*
4255 West Touhy Avenue
Lincolnwood, Illinois 60646–1975 U.S.A.